SKELET

A TEENAGER'S
CLOSET

WHEN FAILURE
BECOMES YOUR
ONLY OPTION,
THEN FAIL BIG

by

Rodney Francis Foster

Gotham Books

30 N Gould St.
Ste. 20820, Sheridan, WY 82801
https://gothambooksinc.com/

Phone: 1 (307) 464-7800

Published by Gotham Books (November 14, 2023)

ISBN: 979-8-88775-515-1 (H)
ISBN: 979-8-88775-513-7 (P)
ISBN: 979-8-88775-514-4 (E)

Based on True to Life Experiences

A MEMOIR

TABLE OF CONTENTS

CHAPTER   **TITLE**   **PAGE**

PART ONE

PIRATES AGAINST THE SEA

(Rules? Hey, I'm only a kid once, ain't I?)

1   WHOOPEE! IT'S EASTER VACATION   4

2   PIRATE EXPLORERS   10

3   SUNKEN TREASURE   16

4   IT TAKES A PLAN   24

5   PIRATES OF THE SEA   29

6   LOST AT SEA   36

7   RESCUED: FRIEND OR FOE   41

8   "FAIL BIG" WHEN YOU FAIL   47

PART TWO

ALFRED AND ME

(Who's disabled?)

9   PICKING UP THE PIECES   51

10   TREASURE OR TROUBLE   56

11   BUCK THE COP AND ALFRED   60

12   A LESSON LEARNED   64

13   WHOOPS!   71

14   SURPRISE! SURPRISE!   75

15   "COUNTRY BUMPKIN"   85

EPILOGUE   THE BULLY/GUNS/RIFLES   99

PART THREE

LITTLE SKELETONS FROM A TEENAGER'S CLOSET
(Not Bad Kids – Maybe Bad Behavior)

FRIENDS ARE BRAVE TOGETHER   104

LET'S SMOKE   105

FIRST CAR - MY MODEL "A"   107

CAVEAT – A WORD TO THE WISE

As a kid I had a wonderful imagination. It continues to this day. Because of this, throughout my life, the books I've read have always been more colorful, more action packed and more interesting than the author probably intended, and certainly much more than movies made from the books. This was, and is a function of my imagination visualizing worlds beyond the written words.

These memoirs are based on actual events from my "formative", preteen and teenage years. Each experience, while based on factual events, is shaped by the wonders of my youthful imagination at the time.

Some portions of the dialogue are not exactly, word for word, the way we said it, but the dialogue communicates the essence of my and my associates' intent.

Beginning with the great depression, these memoirs reflect, in part, the struggle of the "poor middle class", into which I was born, and continues through my family's more prosperous, early "post World War II" years.

Where appropriate, the names and identifying details of some characters in this book have been changed to protect their privacy.

PROLOGUE

Yes, there are lessons to be learned from history, even from those that, at the time, seem to be inconsequential events. In this memoir, I share a concept that now, over half century later, is exemplified by business and government leaders across the country and around the world. **If you are going to fail, then fail BIG.**

Without a basis for comparison, my siblings and I, all depression kids, lived at the poverty level without realizing that our family was only a paycheck away from abject poverty, including loss of food and shelter.

The strain, on my father, of supporting a family that he wasn't sure he wanted, created explosive stress, wherein the smallest infraction of "rules", resulted in corporal punishment, physical abuse. A seemingly benign incident could explode into anger that quickly morphed to rage, wherein the child victims were beaten with a belt or strap, too often causing, in addition to bleeding welts, a backlash of hatred, if only temporary. This was not, in my childhood, an occasional event, but a steady diet of painful punishment that to this day, thinking back, causes me to shudder. Enough that my older brother experienced this type of discipline with me, but to see my sister's bleeding legs following such an event, still exceeds my capacity to forget or fully forgive.

It was an era wherein parents generally believed that if you "spare the rod, you spoil the child". At the time, corporal punishment was considered pretty normal, yet, in our family, it was much too severe, it occurred much too often, and looking back, this "child rearing" disciplinary principle, in my and my siblings' cases, was more than carried to extremes.

And, as one would expect, my siblings and my behaviors were affected by the constant threat of physical abuse, resulting in careful attention to detail related to our relationship, or lack thereof, with our father.

No blame is cast. My father, too, was a victim of the times. There were no manuals or training programs for "parenting". Neighbors "looked the other way". No psychiatrists or psychologists were there offering advice on T.V. talk shows. Parenting practices, including methods of discipline, were very much "family values", handed down from one generation to the next, based on the culture and experiences within each family group.

While I still cannot understand, and never could recommend this extreme, if unforgivable, parental action with children, as I view the world today, with the increasingly irresponsible behavior among many youths, and adults, I am more inclined to believe that the lessons we, my siblings and I learned "from the belt", while well beyond any of the "norms" of the time, and painful to endure, resulted in the four of us becoming responsible adults and caring parents.

A child will sometimes grow up wishing to be exactly like a loved parent. And, a child will grow up, making every effort to be exactly the opposite of a hated parent. So, it is.

CHAPTER 1: WHOOPEE! IT'S EASTER VACATION

Easter week! It's the best. School's out! Dad has to work.

The best is that I have the whole week to do whatever I like. Even better is that my uncle Tex, Mom's youngest brother, will be here. He's a year older than I. He lives on the farm in Williams with Grandpa and Grandma. He's a farmer. I live in Pinole with my older brother, Duane and my younger siblings, Bruce and Belva. We're "city dudes".

Mom's younger sister, Zella, lives just two houses from us. Tex gets to see two of his three sisters during his annual visit.

Tex has always lived on a farm. Every day is an adventure for him. When he's here on Easter week, we have the time of our lives. We explore places and do things I would never think of in a thousand years.

Dad's pretty strict. I get the belt every time I come close to breaking a rule. I don't care that much when I'm with Tex.

I'm in the fifth grade at Pinole school. Duane is in the eighth grade. We've gone to Pinole school since I was in kindergarten and Duane was in third grade. Duane has always been my mentor and role model. He's the best "big brother" I could ever wish for.

Duane and I are going to meet Tex at the bus station this Saturday morning. He is about Duane's size, and an inch taller than I. He seems like he's much older, but he's only in the sixth grade.

On the farm Tex works like a regular hand. He's in the 4-H and has his own herd of cows. Well, two cows. He milks them twice a day. He's got some chickens, a sheep, a goat and a couple of pigs. He tends to all of his livestock and helps Grandma and Grandpa with all the chores on the farm.

Tex's five brothers and three sisters are older than he is. Except for his sister, Melba, who is a teenager, all his brothers and sisters left the farm and are out on their own.

Mom usually lets Duane and me spend summers on the farm with Tex and our grandparents. All year long, there are so many chores to do that Tex has only this one-week of vacation to visit Mom, his oldest sister, and play with his nephews and nieces.

There's no studying and no work for any of us for a whole week. Tex, Duane and I will be the "Three Musketeers".

Tex arrives at the bus station, right on schedule, early Saturday morning. With Duane, I take my paneled red wagon to the station to meet him. It's only five blocks from our house. We figure we can haul his bags in the wagon, and maybe even Tex if he wants a rest after the long bus trip.

No way. When the bus stops and the door opens, he jumps clean out, never touching a step. He grabs me. Duane grabs him. We hug and slap and jump all over the place.

The bus driver yells, "Hey, you kids gonna take this bag or does it go on with me?"

We rush for the open baggage door and grab Tex's suitcase. It's got straps and a piece of rope holding it closed. Looks like it came west on a covered wagon. Probably did.

We cross the bridge over the creek as we walk toward home. Tex stops and looks down at the "white water". The early spring runoff is rushing through the culvert and on down stream to the bay.

"Hey you guys, we've got to explore this river out to the bay. I'll bet the fish are fighting each other to get upstream and spawn. We can prob'ly catch some."

Tex knows all about fishing and hunting. That's where most of the food comes from on the farm. He's a real sharpshooter with a rifle and a shotgun, too.

Upstream a ways, I cross the creek, jumping from rock to rock most every day on my way to school. When the water is this high, I have to go the long way and cross the bridge. A couple of times I've shown up at school wetter and muddier than a pig in a slough after missing a rock as I crossed.

Duane and I, like Tex, love adventure. He says, "With a whole week, we can search back up the valley for the start of the creek and then search for treasures all the way to the bay, and we can start today."

The creek begins in the hills beyond the valley, runs through town, splitting it in two, then goes on a couple of miles to the bay. Mom buys her milk from a dairy up the valley, so we've been there in a car, but never all the way along the creek on foot. There's lots of water this time of year.

I respond, "I'm not sure. Maybe we can just go up the road and find where the creek starts. It gets pretty deep and even deeper down by the bay." I almost drowned in a lake accident a couple of years ago and if it weren't for Tex I would have. I'm not crazy about deep water. In fact, I'm downright scared.

We were having a family picnic at Clear Lake with all of Mom's relatives. Dad rented a rowboat to take all the kids for a ride. It cost a buck and that's almost half of what he made in a day at work in the sugar refinery. You could tell that Mom didn't really agree with him, but he did it anyway. I guess she figured he didn't spend much time with us kids and this might be good for all of us.

Six of us kids piled into the boat with my dad, and away we went, everyone taking turns at the oars. There was a little wind so the lake was pretty choppy. I sat in the back and held on. I was the only one in the boat that couldn't swim. I just never liked deep water. Mom always said to just be patient and I'd learn.

We'd been out on the lake for almost four hours. Dad had to return the boat or pay extra. He knew Mom wouldn't like that. We were getting pretty close to shore when suddenly I felt dad's hands lifting me.

"Splash", I was in the water.

He yelled, "Son, it's time you learned to swim!"

I sunk. Tried to breath and couldn't. Water everywhere. All I could see was the dirty water. I could feel myself sinking. No air! I was scared to death. I knew it was all over.

Then I felt a tug – something was pulling my arm. I gagged, closed my eyes and "went to sleep".

Later, coughing up water, eyes and nose running, laid out on the beach, I found out that Tex had jumped in after me and swimming with one arm, pulling me with the other, had gotten me close to shore. Mom and my Aunt Melba, screaming, had dragged me out of the water. Everyone worked on me until all the water I'd swallowed was gone and I could breathe.

Dad didn't say much after that. Mom and her brothers and sisters were about to kill him. From that day on I was really careful to stay away from deep water.

"Hey, no problem! I saved you once – I'll just do it again." Tex is laughing. I'm embarrassed.

"Okay, if you guys can do it, I can, too."

We arrive home. Mom's got breakfast on the table. Tex grabs her and gives her a big hug. He's at home anywhere.

We are just finishing our pancakes when he looks over at Mom. "Sis, will you make a few sandwiches for us? We're going to be walking all over town and the valley so I'll remember where everything is. We'll probably be gone all day."

I stare at Tex, a little surprised. Duane's eating pancakes like there's no tomorrow. We don't have pancakes often. I figured we'd just do our exploring without anyone knowing what we're doing.

Mom worries a lot about us, ever since my older sister died. She was born at home with a midwife. She was a "baby in a veil" and there was nothing the midwife or any of the family could do to save her. By the time they got to the doctor it was too late. She lived a few days, but the damage had been done. I don't think Mom ever really recovered. She's pretty comfortable with Tex, though. She knows he's on his own a lot on the farm and is a lot more adult than his years.

She agrees to make the sandwiches and tells us to be home for dinner. I'm thinking, "My God, what if Dad found out we're going to explore the creek all the way to the bay? It would be the belt, for sure." He's been trying to find an excuse to use the belt on Tex ever since Grandpa "beat the crap" out of Duane.

That was really a crazy one. It's been years but I remember it like it was yesterday.

We are at Grandpa's farm for the summer. The apples, now ripe, are falling from the trees so Tex is showing us how they make apple cider. He's never actually done it, but has helped. Here we are at the cider press with a bunch of apples on the ground, just waiting to be "squished" into juice. There's a "funnel" at the top of the press where the apples go in, then you crank the press like an old car and the "screws" catch the apples pushing and squeezing them toward the "filter" at the end and out comes the juice. The rest of the apple just drops away onto the ground.

Tex shows us how it works. He puts his finger into the press like an apple dropping into the screws. He cranks the press. Whap! His finger is caught like an apple on its way to becoming cider. He screams – loud!

Well, Grandpa hears the scream and comes a runn'in. By the time he gets there Duane's got the crank and reverses it to loosen its grip on Tex's finger. You guessed! Grandpa thinks he ground Tex's finger in the press. Off with his belt and he beats him nearly to death. Tex is hurting too much to say anything. I'm too scared to say anything. When Grandpa finally stops my brother is a mess.

It isn't until later at dinner, which my brother misses, that Tex finally is able to tell Grandpa what really happened. I don't think that Duane, to this day, has forgiven Grandpa. I know Dad hasn't.

We go to my room so Tex can unpack.

CHAPTER 2 - PIRATE EXPLORERS

Tex immediately begins. "We'll be explorers. Like Lewis and Clark. First, we'll go downstream to the bay. We'll search for treasures along the way. We'll need some good sticks to smack any fish we see. Sis will really be surprised if we bring a big fish home for dinner. Maybe we can even take a swim in the bay."

Duane jumps on like it's his own idea. I'm not sure. Since my scare at the Clear Lake picnic, I've learned to "dog paddle" at the Richmond natatorium, but I stay close to the edge. I still don't really like swimming and not in the bay. And, the creek is pretty deep in places this time of year. I'm okay exploring the creek but don't want to do any swimming in the bay.

I pop up, "Okay with me. We've never been all the way down to the bay. I'll just pass on the swimming."

"No problem Boomie." Tex loves to call me by my nickname. He and just a few others in the family know why I got such a strange name. "You can stand watch and make sure no one sneaks up on us. And guard our treasures. Who knows what we'll have by then?"

We're ready to go in no time. Mom has the sandwiches bagged. We head out. I put the food in my backpack. Mom gives us bottles of water. They go in with the sandwiches. Tex wears his farm boots and we "city dudes" wear our tennis shoes. We know we'll get wet, but we've done that before. The creek is just a couple of blocks from our house. There's a well-worn path right next to Jim Bradley's house to the creek. Jim's three years older than I and is one of Duane's classmates. I love to "hang out" with them.

When the water is low, I jump from rock to rock to cross the creek without getting my feet wet. Today none of us care. We know we'll be wading most of the way where the banks of the creek are overgrown with brush and berries. We're excited as we begin our journey.

From where we are the creek flows through town, then across a wasteland north of town until it reaches the bay. There are three giant culverts that carry the water under a bridge in the center of town. That's the bridge we crossed with Tex earlier. It's about two miles from town to the bay.

Tex leads the way through the willows and berry bush overgrowth alongside the water. Duane follows and I'm happy to be last.

Just minutes later Tex yells, "watch out". At the same time I hear the thud. Duane gets it right in the face, knocking him over and into the water. A branch Tex bent to get by got loose from his grip and, like a whip, springs back into place. Duane is in that place. He gets it, full force.

Tex rushes back to Duane who is splashing water like a drowning duck, trying to get to his feet. I don't see blood. A wave of relief! During some of our adventures together, I've already seen too much of Duane's blood.

"Man, I'm sorry." Tex is all over Duane, making sure he's okay.

Duane brushes off the water and mud. There's a big red welt across his cheek. "No problem. Lesson learned. I'll remember not to tail so close behind you."

Lesson for me, too. That could just as easily have been me. And I'm carrying the sandwiches and water. We spread out to about ten feet, single file, Duane following Tex and me still bringing up the rear. Mostly we walk along the edge of the creek, but now and then there is no way to pass through the growth on the sides, so we wade down the center, water up to our knees; sometimes up to my waist. The current is pretty strong. I'm nervous, but try to hide it.

We reach the culverts in the center of town. Tex and Duane are getting confident. Now we're Pirates. These are secret caves. Each cave is about six feet in diameter. The water is running fast, about two feet deep in each one.

Tex chooses the center cave to explore. I totally forget about the times I've stood on the bridge above to watch the water flow out the ends like a waterfall. It drops about five feet into a pool where the creek continues its journey toward the bay. Around the bridge there's a chain link fence to keep people from being down here. Following our secret passage along the creek bed we've avoided the fence, something the "adults" obviously didn't consider. Pirates are sneaky.

The overgrowth covering the entrance to the cave is so thick it's almost like night as we enter.

Tex says, "Hey, we need a torch. I can't see in here."

Limbs partially block the opposite end of the cave. I can barely see Tex's outline as he raises his hands to move the limbs. He disappears.

Duane enters the cave behind him. I follow. It's dark. Duane stops. I stop. We can't see Tex. There's a huge splash ahead.

We hear Tex's voice. "Stop! Stop! Don't take another step."

I can hear splashing in front of me. We carefully move ahead. Duane and I are now standing together on the spot where we last saw Tex. It's then that I remember the falls, and the drop over the edge.

"Tex, are you okay? What happened?" Duane's voice.

I feel like an idiot. Why didn't I think about this? My tongue won't work. I can't bring myself to say a word.

Tex shouts again, "Nothing broken but it's a helluva first step out of the cave. Gotta be a better way to get down here!"

Duane, ever the brave explorer, moves up a couple of steps and leans over the edge. Tex is below, still making thrashing noises in the water. Duane calls, "Hey Tex, how deep is it down there?"

Tex is now standing with water up to his chest. "About four feet."
"Any rocks?" My gosh! Duane is thinking of jumping off the edge. I
can't believe I'm hearing this.

"No, just a little muddy on the bottom."

"You're not going to do what I'm thinking are you brother?"

Duane turns to me. No fear! He's been through so much he's game
for anything. "It's not that far down there. Like diving into the pool.
Maybe four or five feet! We do that all summer."

I know it's more.

"It'd take us forever to backtrack up the creek. Water will break the
fall. No problem." He lets out a mighty yell and jumps.

I see the splash as he hits. Water everywhere. I'm alone in the cave.
I'm not thinking much about Pirates. I look back. Maybe I can find a
way to get over the fence. No way. It's got rolled barbed wire all
along the top. I move a step forward. There's Tex and Duane, both
standing in the water waving and yelling for me to follow.

I think of the huge slide at Playland and the thrill of the swift descent
from top to bottom. I think of drowning in Clear Lake. I think of our
experience in the culvert last summer. I think of flying to Mars in my
orange crate rocket ship. My feet are cold and wet and my forehead
is covered with beads of hot sweat.

Finally I lean out and throw the backpack to Tex. He catches it. They
move back and signal for me to jump.

I think of the World's Fair last year and the divers who dove from
the hundred-foot platform into the pool. There was hardly a splash
as they "cut" the water, headfirst. Nope, I'm going feet first. In fact,
I'm going "cannon-ball". I stand still, fists clenched. I take one last
look at the water below. Eyes closed, teeth grinding, I leap out into
space and grab my knees, pulling them close to my chest. I'm
hanging in thin air. It seems like forever. I open my eyes just as I hit

the water like a giant rock. Water in my eyes, up my nose and in my mouth! Mud everywhere. I hit bottom with a thud. I can't see a thing.

Then I feel hands groping at me and pulling me up. I'm alive. Sputtering and spitting water and mud I finally get up on my feet. The water is almost to my shoulders. I'm standing on the tips of my toes.

"Great dive!" It's Tex holding onto my arm, making sure I don't slip under again.

I force a laugh. "Hey, that was fun. Maybe we should do it again." I'm shaking, more from fright than being cold and wet.

Duane pipes in. "Since we're wet let's just explore right down the middle of the creek. We can't get any wetter. And maybe we'll find some treasures in the water."

"Sounds great to me." Tex has adventure running through his veins.

"I'm game. Tex, you can carry the backpack. It'll get wet if I fall down."

Courageous Pirates, we stumble along through the undergrowth and water, one step at a time. We watch for rocks and deep pools as we wade toward the bay. The undergrowth is thinning. The creek widens as we get nearer to our goal. The water is about to our knees with little current. The silt is about a foot deep. It almost pulls my shoes off with every step. Tex is still our front man but we're pretty well bunched up in a single file procession.

"Hey, I can see the bay." Tex has moved a few steps ahead of us and is standing on something that's under the water.

Duane splashes forward at a waddling jog. I follow. Just as he reaches Tex he stumbles forward, face down into the water. His shoes, covered with mud almost hit me in the face as he falls. I stop. Water is splashing every which direction as a face and head, covered with mud, rise up out of the water.

"What happened? Is there a hole there?" I'm standing still. Tex is helping Duane to his feet.

Sputtering, Duane says, "I tripped. Must be roots or something under there."

Water is dripping out of his nose and mouth as he speaks. He's wiping mud off his face as he shakes his head. Mud's flying everywhere. I'm not making a move till I know what's going on.

CHAPTER 3 - SUNKEN TREASURE

It's not deep but the water is so muddy we can't see the bottom. I inch forward, a small half step at a time. Tex is feeling around under the water where Duane fell. Duane goes to the bank and tries to wipe some of the mud off with loose grass.

My foot bumps something solid and I stop. "There's something under here, where I'm standing."

Tex moves toward me, very slowly. He drags one hand and arm under the water. He squats, moving his hand back and forth. "Feels like boards. Some kind of platform or something."

He now has both hands under the water and is lifting hands full of mud up from the bottom. Crouched in the grass on the bank Duane looks like a muddy frog about to leap into the water.

"Hey, let me have the backpack before you go under too." I take the backpack with our sandwiches to Duane as Tex continues his underwater search.

It's still morning but it's been a couple of hours since we started. I'm ready for a sandwich. "Let's eat one of our sandwiches now. It'll only take a few minutes to get from here to the bay." Wading through the water is work. I'm tired and hungry.

"Good idea but we've got to dig this thing up." Tex pulls up one last handful of mud. "After we eat we can all dig. It's kinda round and smooth. Could be a treasure chest lost from a ship." He's still a pirate searching for treasure.

Duane's back in the water washing mud from his head and face. He's a mess. There's so much silt in the water that he doesn't make much progress. Actually, Tex and I aren't much better with the stuff all over our hands and arms. Finally, we all have enough of the mud off our hands to see bare skin. We unwrap our sandwiches, laughing and joking about the adventures we've shared so far.

We're not in any hurry so we explore some of the area around the creek bank while we're eating.

We decide to rest for a few minutes before tackling the mud to find out what's under the water. When we visit the farm, we always take a short nap after a meal so we're ready for the work ahead.

I guess we all doze off for a few minutes, for the sun is quite a bit higher in the sky when I feel Tex shaking me. Duane's still asleep on his back, strange noises coming from his mouth. He wakes up very slowly. I watch while Tex shakes him awake.

We don't know anything about the bay, or the ocean, and the waves and tides. All of Tex's and our water experience has been in the lakes in Lake County or in the irrigation canals up in the Sacramento Valley where Tex, Grandpa and Grandma live. Like me, Duane has never been down the creek this close to the bay.

Summers, between chores, Tex, Duane and I explore miles around the farms and ranches by wading and crawling along through the irrigation water in the canals. Sometimes we're "Navy Frogmen" on a secret mission. Other times we're on Mars exploring the "Red Planet". Tex is a great adventurer so we explore whatever place or wherever he wants to go.

Last summer was a real experience. We get up with the sun and help Tex so morning chores are finished early. Dressed in our swimsuits, we set out to find the hidden gold mines among the canals feeding the Sacramento River. Of course, these are the irrigation ditches that feed water to the rice fields.

We enter the first canal right in front of Grandpa's farm where the water is about two feet deep. It is flowing north toward our great uncle Dee's rice ranch. Sometimes great uncle Dee hires us, at ten cents a day, to round up his livestock. He is pretty tight with his money.

On this day we decide to follow this branch of the river through town, about a quarter of a mile north, then take the main fork west where there are several feeder streams. There's a small spillway where the feeders come together to keep fish from swimming upstream. The gold mines we are searching for are just past the spillway. Our canal flows through a long culvert under the road as it passes through town on the way to the spillway.

About half-hour later, mostly crawling and paddling in the shallow water we are at the culvert. On days when the water is too deep, we just get out and walk over the road and get back into the canal. Today there is plenty of room to "hunch over" and crawl along with the current, under the road and we'll be on the other side. We're explorers and this is a cave to be explored.

There's a gate with bars at the end of the culvert to catch stuff so the irrigation gates at the spillway won't get blocked. There's a big latch on the culvert gate to open it and clean whatever has been caught. People who work for the irrigation district come by and do this a couple of times a day. We plan to just open the gate and slip through. If there's any good stuff caught in the gate, we'll take it with us. We'll leave the other stuff behind.

It's dark in these culverts with just a speck of light at each end. We start our "journey through the cave" with Tex in front, then Duane and me following. I stay close so I can see Duane and Tex clearly in front of me.

We barely get started into the "cave" and I hear a kinda loud "swishing" noise behind us. I'm afraid to turn around and lose sight of Duane and Tex, but the noise keeps getting louder. Finally I can't resist and turn around. What I see almost makes me pee. There is a wall of water coming at us – and it is going to hit the culvert in just a minute.

What we forgot is that when they open water gates to supply irrigation water to additional farmers, sometimes the canals fill up fast – right to the top. That's what is happening – and we are in the culvert.

Finally, I yell, "Duane - Tex! Water! Water!"

Tex looks and yells, "Let's go – quick!"

Tex grabs Duane who grabs me and we try to run through the water that is already up to our waist. The culvert is filling fast. It'll be over our head in just a minute. The current helps move us toward the end but the water keeps getting deeper, with barely room for our heads between the water and the top of the culvert. Tex is at the gate struggling to find the latch. It is under water level and on the outside of the bars. He takes a deep breath and dives under like a frogman.

Duane helps me stay erect. We lean our heads back so we can breathe in the small space remaining between the rising water and the top of the culvert. The water is still rising – up to our ears. I know we are goners, for sure. We've lost Tex.

Just as the water is about to cover our faces, we take a deep breath and go under, just like Tex had. There he is, squished up against the gate, the handle of the gate in one hand, his other on a bar – pulling on the handle with everything he has. Duane grabs the end of the handle with Tex and just like that, the gate opens. My lungs are about to bust – I know Tex has been under water longer than Duane or I. Then, like a ball shot from a cannon we are on the other side. Air!

Our expedition ends, right there. Pretty subdued, we walk the halfmile back to the farm. By the time we get there Tex is laughing and joking about the "tidal wave". I am still shaking with "aftershock".

That summer we have lots of "canal expeditions", but don't take any "shortcuts" through "caves" again.

Anyway, today we are about to get our first lesson in tides. While we've eaten our sandwiches and taken a rest the tide has been going out and the level of water in the creek has been dropping.

Tex is first to notice. "Look at the water you guys. It's getting shallow and I can see the platform we found."

Sure enough, near the middle of the creek there's something beginning to show from under the now shallower water. We're so close to the bay that as the tide goes out it lowers the water level in the creek. We watch for a few minutes. A wooden platform gradually rises an inch, then another inch.

"This isn't a platform." Duane has waded out to the object and is scraping mud from it. "This thing is curved. It looks like the bottom of a boat."

Excited? Tex and I are in the water in a flash, helping Duane pull the mud off of our find.

Tex is almost completely under water, feeling the shape. "It is a boat. It's upside down. Let's see if we can turn it over."

The water continues to disappear as the bay tide goes out and the shape of the boat comes into almost full view. We're working feverishly to remove the scum and mud to get a good look at our treasure. There's mud everywhere. I can barely tell who is Tex and who is Duane. We get the boat to shift a bit as we all lift from one side. We keep lifting but it's stuck on something and won't budge. I'm beginning to think we'll never get it up.

"Rubber Darts!" It's Tex. "I know what's wrong. You know how a rubber dart sticks to the board when you shoot it? Suction. This boat is like a big dart and suction is holding it down. Just like a dart, we've got to get one edge up and let air in to break the suction."

I don't understand. Duane does. "Yeah, that's okay but how do we do that? We can't budge it and there's water all around it."

Tex is not deterred. "Man, it's easy. We just get a piece of hollow pipe and slip it under the edge of the boat. Let some air in and just like that the suction's gone."

Doubting, Duane again. "Okay my wise friend. But where do we get a piece of hollow pipe out here?"

Tex stands with a puzzled look on his face. Duane is staring at him. I'm thinking.

"I've got it." They turn and look at me with skeptical amazement. "Bean shooters. We make bean shooters out of the reeds from down here by the creek. They're hollow and some of them are two feet long. There are only a couple of inches of water left. We can use a bean shooter like a pipe."

Disbelief! Tex looks at Duane. Duane looks at Tex and then back at me. They both begin laughing crazily.

"That's a great idea, Boomie. We've been wading through reeds all morning." Tex takes out his knife and we begin our search for a long reed. In a few minutes we have one that's almost three feet long with over an inch wide hole. We're in business.

Back at our boat we're ready for our recovery plan. "Great. Now how do we get it through the water and mud and under the boat without it clogging up?" I'm not so sure about my idea now.

Tex is up to the task. He carves a small plug from a piece of reed and sticks it into the end of our pipe. "We just dig out the mud from under the edge of the boat. When I feel the other side I'll just stick the pipe in, plugged end first. We can push the plug out with a smaller reed from this end and 'wham' the suction is gone and we'll be able to turn it over."

Complex solutions for the simplest of problems!

Duane's got it first. "Hey Tex, the water is gone from this side of the boat. When we dig through the mud under this side, that will break the suction. No need for the pipe." While we were doing our thing finding a "pipe", the tide had gone out enough that we were now faced with just mud.

Eureka! We start digging with our hands. Since we're above the water line now we soon hear air as the suction breaks. Six hands on the edge of the boat and we've got it on it's side, then upright.

21

"Wow! It's in pretty good shape. I'll bet it's seaworthy." Tex is ready to float it.

The "ship" is about eight feet long and about four feet wide. I grab hold and help slide it across the mud and part way up the bank of the creek. It's a real treasure. Our "pirate's ship"! "It's a two seater." Tex kicks the two cross section planks. "Hey, it's a three seater. There's a place to sit at the back end." It's Duane. We're so excited we can't even count.

We're now furiously scraping mud off the hull with our hands. Tex is busy checking the sides and bottom of the boat. When most of the mud is gone from the inside we pull our "ship" further up on our "dock", away from the water line.

"Let's turn it over so we can see if there are any holes in the hull." It's Tex. He's anxious to get our ship into the water.

First we make sure we've got it far enough from the water that the incoming tide won't "sink" it again. Then we all grab the side and role it over. For the first time we can see the hull with just a little mud left.

We inspect every board. Some are a little loose. Some have small cracks where the tongue and groove has rotted away. One has come loose at the end and is sticking out like a broken arm in a cast.

We've been so excited we haven't even noticed that the sun is beginning to set.

"Hey you guys, we've got to get back home. If Dad beats us there you know what that'll mean." Dad will be off work in a while and it only takes him about half an hour to get home.

Tex doesn't understand. He's from a different world. "Let's just look around and find some stuff to fix the holes before we leave our ship." We're pirates. We have our ship. Tex is ready and wants to set sail.

I quickly explain what happens if we're late and have to tell Dad what we've been doing and why we're so mucked up.

Tex doesn't want to "feel the belt" any more than we. He agrees to get home, right now. We know what we'll need to "make her seaworthy" so we take off on a dead run across the wetlands for home.

CHAPTER 4 – IT TAKES A PLAN

Mom's in the front yard waiting for us as we run down the street to our house. By the time Tex, Duane and I are around back and on the porch Mom has the bathtub full and waiting. She's not afraid of Dad, but she hates the beatings almost as much as we.

She saw plenty while she was growing up. Her father, Grandpa, could be pretty fierce with animals and kids when they "broke the rules". He once got so mad at one of his horses that he went into a crazy rage and beat it to death with a chain.

It was winter. I was only five years old. Grandpa and Grandma had moved to Round Valley where they rented a dairy farm. Like always, Grandpa, who loved horses, had two, a buckskin and a blue, for his personal riding. He kept a couple of really gentle horses for us kids to ride.

Mom's next younger brother, with his wife and son had also moved to Round Valley to try their luck at dairy farming. Mom and Dad decided to do the same, but instead of milking cows, they decided to "crop farm". I remember that when winter came it was awful. Snow everywhere. The dairies did okay, but the summer had been dry, so our crops weren't much. Dad returned to Crockett where he went back to work for the C & H Sugar Refinery. The rest of us stayed in the valley until he had enough money to rent a house and send for us.

We were snowed in the valley for six weeks. In the middle of winter everyone except Mom got the flu and were too sick to do anything. Right then Mom went to the little clinic where my baby sister was born. Well, sick as he was, Grandpa tended to the livestock. It was pretty tough going.

In the middle of a rainstorm Grandpa went out to feed and water the horses. They'd been kept in the barn to protect them from the weather. He had to take the horses across the corral, which was knee deep with sticky mud and manure, to get to the watering trough. He'd watered the buckskin and had the blue in halter, leading him across the corral.

The blue was always kind of skittish, but in this weather and muck he bolted, knocking Grandpa down. Already not feeling well, this really made Grandpa mad. He dug himself out of the mire. Then back at the barn he got a length of chain and came back to the corral to show the blue a thing or two. With the length of chain, he began beating the blue around the head. With every stroke Grandpa got madder. In the muck the horse couldn't move any better than Grandpa. Each time the horse tried to get away Grandpa was there with the chain.

Pretty soon the horse was down. Grandpa quit the beating. It was too late. His prize blue stallion was dead.

Over the years I've learned that this wild rage runs in our family. I know it doesn't take much for Dad to get just about as mad. My brothers, sister and I have talked about this a lot. We've all promised each other, and ourselves, that we'll never "lose it and cry" during one of these beatings. It doesn't always work.

We're bathed and in clean clothes by the time Dad is home and dinner is ready.

"You boys manage to stay out of trouble today?" A typical question from Dad! We usually don't talk much at the dinner table. Too much risk! And Dad likes to get dinner over with so he can read. When he's not working, he's always got his "nose in a book". Mom doesn't like to read so Dad's reading sometimes causes a little tension. Dad had to quit school when he was in the sixth grade to help support his mother. His dad went to the store one day for groceries and just disappeared. I guess Dad's love of reading now makes up for his not being able to go to school like the other kids.

Tex responds to Dad immediately. I'm holding my breath. "We had a great time exploring the valley all up and down the creek. We might try to do a little fishing in some of the pools tomorrow".

Dad grunts. "Well, better be careful. Lots of water this time of year. We don't need any drowned kids."

I look pleadingly at Tex. He gets the message and goes back to eating dinner. I, with a sigh of relief, finish my dinner.

"Can we be excused?" Around our house, you don't dare leave the dinner table until Dad excuses you.

Dad mumbles between bites, "Okay." It's almost 7:30 and we have to be in bed by 8:00. We want to get all of the "stuff" we'll need for our ship tonight, so we can get an early start tomorrow. Dad leaves for work at six in the morning.

As we're leaving the room Tex, ever a bit brash asks Dad, "Mr. Foster, is it okay if we use your hammer and hand saw? We want to fix up the 'box scooter' and maybe build another". Tex is learning. He'd never "stretch the truth" like this with Grandpa.

"Just put the tools back where they belong when you're done." Again, I let out a sigh of relief. It could have gone the other way and we'd be in the basement, not with tools but with the belt.

Minutes later in the basement, we've retrieved several short pieces of scrap lumber from our store of wood that's used to fire the kitchen stove. We find a few nails and the hammer and saw. We're ready for tomorrow's adventure.

I'm excited but still not quite comfortable with sailing in our "ship". I'm thinking about all those small holes where the tongue and groove sides have rotted. "How are we going to fix all the little holes on the sides of our ship?" I'm thinking out loud. We have enough pieces of lumber to nail over the large holes. But it could even leak around our patches.

Silence. I've gotten Tex's attention. Ever the optimist Tex exclaims, "How about just packing some mud in the cracks and let it dry. They're small and it will probably hold pretty good!"

Tex can see that I'm skeptical. Then I smile. "Hey, how about some paste? We make paste out of flour and water all the time for school projects. Why not do the same for the cracks in the boat?" I'm thinking. To dissolve our flour and water paste we just use more water and it's gone. Then I add, "We need something to fill the cracks that won't wash away with water like mud or paste will."

Tex is looking around the basement. I'm checking all the cans that Dad has stored on the shelves. I'm thinking.

All at once two voices! Tex whispers, "Putty." Duane almost shouts, "Clay!"

I find a gallon container of putty that's about half full on the shelf. I think of the clay that Duane and I each got last Christmas that's been stored in our toy box for months.

Tex again. "Great idea. Let's take both. If the clay doesn't work, we can use the putty. Maybe use both, together. We may have discovered a new way to repair boats."

We're all excited as we realize it's almost eight o'clock, bedtime. We've gotta get out of here.

"One more thing." Tex is standing with hands on hips, thoughtfully. "Just in case, we should have something to bail water out of our ship if we spring a small leak."

Sure enough, there are several empty two-pound coffee cans lined up along the workbench. Dad uses them to store screws, nails and such. We set two aside with the lumber, hammer, putty, nails and saw. All set, we make it upstairs barely in time to "hit the sack" by bedtime.

It's eight o'clock and we're in bed. That's the rule. It doesn't matter whether it's a school night or not, were in bed by eight o'clock. I share a bed with Duane and Tex is using a cot Dad moved in from my sister's bedroom. She has a single bed and the cot is for her girlfriends who stay over. She agreed. No girlfriends over this week!

In bed but none of us can sleep. We're ready to launch our ship. Tex is talking about sailing through the Golden Gate into the ocean. Up the coast, landing on a beach and exploring for buried treasure.

I'm between excited and scared. I haven't been on a boat since I nearly drowned in Clear Lake. But that was because I was thrown into the water. Now I'll have both Tex and Duane to look out for me. Besides, I've learned to "dog paddle" so it's not so bad. I'm beginning to share Tex's excitement.

Pretty soon Mom comes in to warn us that we'd better get some sleep. What she's really saying is that if we don't shut up, we'll probably get a visit from Dad. She puts our clean clothes on a chair and leaves. A couple more whispers and we conk out. It's been a long day.

CHAPTER 5 - PIRATES OF THE SEA

I'm shaking! Slowly I open my eyes. It's Tex. He's up and dressed. The clock says 5:30. It's still dark. Tex is used to getting up early and milking his cows and tending to the farm chores.

"Hey man, you gonna sleep all day?" He shakes me again. A mumble and groan. I don't always wake up that fast. School days Duane and I usually have to run so we're not late for first class.

Suddenly I jump up in bed; eyes wide open. "Man, I've been dreaming about sailing in our new ship. The wind was taking us east and we were paddling as hard as we could to go west. Just kept going east up the Delta with the wind."

"Paddling!" It's Tex. "We need some oars."

I'm awake and up now. I shake Duane. A groan. "How about a shovel? Dad's got a round one, a square one and one with a short handle."

I'm sitting on the bed, fully awake, "Maybe just one shovel. If anything happens to any of Dad's tools it'll really be our butts."

"Settled! One shovel will work swell. We'll just row on one side then the other. No problem." Tex is ready to go. Duane, yawning, is getting dressed.

By the time Mom's made breakfast and sandwiches for our lunch, Dad is gone to work so we eat, pack our lunch, hit the basement for our supplies and we're off, through our back yard to the fence, double time out the gate, down the sidewalk, through town and then across the open field to our ship.

The tide must be in when we arrive, for the water is up to our waist as we wade across the creek to our ship. It's right at the waterline. I start digging all the mud out of the inside. Tex fits the short lumber pieces over the most gaping holes, marks them and Duane saws them so they are long enough to cover. I'm using the putty to fill all the little cracks on the inside of the hull. Tex is using our clay to cover the cracks from the outside of the hull. We're finished in no time.

I pack our lunch, the bailing cans and our "oar" into the now "fully repaired" hull.

"It looks good." Tex is inspecting his and Duane's repairs. He's added some putty around the patches. I've got my eyeballs closely searching the inside, looking for any light coming through.

"Well, the bottom looks okay. The boards on the back are a little loose." I give them my report.

Tex and Duane do their own inspection. "Boomie's right. We need to nail a support to hold up the rear seat or it might fall down and leave a hole in the back of the hull." Tex already has a board measured. Duane saws the piece off and they nail it into place.

We're ready to launch. It's only eight o'clock. The sun has just come up and is shining on the water. It's a beautiful, quiet day. Even the mud in the creek seems shallower.

We put the extra pieces of wood into the ship, along with the tools, the putty and clay and the rest of the nails. Just in case.

"What do they say when they launch a ship?" It's Tex, ready to push her into the water.

"Our ship's got to have a name." Duane's right. We can't launch a ship without a name.

"Let's name her Old Patch and launch her with a Ship Ahoy." I put in my two cents worth.

It's done. We all yell "Ship Ahoy" as our new ship, "Old Patch", slides down the bank and into the creek. I jump inside while Duane and Tex stay behind and push the ship and me down the creek with the current.

Sailing through the creek, water must be washing some of the mud from the bottom of the ship. I see a couple of 'seeping' leaks next to my feet. Everything else seems to be holding okay.

"We've got a leak in the bottom." Duane and Tex are having so much fun pushing the ship toward the bay they haven't even thought to look for leaks. Tex wades around to the side and looks at the leaks near my feet.

"No problem. They'll probably go away as soon as the boards get wet enough and swell. Leaks like that happen every time our watering troughs go dry and we fill them again for the cattle." Tex knows so much. I'm impressed. They aren't leaking very fast. We've still got some clay and putty, just in case.

What I don't know is, what is going to happen when we reach the bay and Tex and Duane both get into our ship with me.

We can see the waves from the bay about a hundred yards ahead. The water is almost to Tex 's chest now. Duane holds one side while Tex climbs in the other. Then Tex climbs over me and takes Duane's hand.

"Whoa! We're going to sink." I'm shouting. Tex and Duane's weight on one side is too much. We're taking water over the side.

Tex backs off. I start bailing with the coffee can. Duane wades around to the back of the ship and crawls on board from the rear. Well, we're learning. Now we know we need to keep the weight in the ship even.

I settle in the middle and hang onto the seat. Duane sits on the front seat. Tex is in the back with the shovel, our "oar". The current and tide are taking us out the mouth of the creek into the waves of the bay. Tex uses the "oar" like a rudder to keep us from turning sideways.

We're in the bay with the current from the creek now behind us. Our ship stops going forward and begins to turn sideways. It starts to rock as the waves hit the side.

31

I'm getting nervous. We're only thirty or forty feet from the shoreline but the waves seem like a giant tsunami to me. Tex is struggling with the "oar" to get us going straight into the waves. Duane, in front of me, is leaning over the side, paddling with his hand. The tide is still coming in and each wave is bigger than the last.

"Let's just turn toward the shore and let the waves push us in." I've had enough of this adventure. I'm ready for dry land. Some water from the waves is beginning to splash over the side.

"Hey, Boomie, no problem. If you and Duane both get one of the sticks and paddle, we can have the ship straight in no time." Tex is paddling like crazy from the back.

Duane already has a stick about two feet long, and is busy paddling. Neither he nor Tex seems to be concerned with our condition. I get a stick and begin to paddle right behind Duane. Sure enough, the ship comes around and we're moving, very slowly, into the waves.

"Boomie, why don't you get a can and bail out any water that comes over the side. Duane and I will keep the ship straight and sailing into the waves." Tex is gaining confidence with every minute. I look at him, expecting to see a pirate's cap, an eye patch and a hook arm. He's a pirate and we're on an adventure.

Pretty soon the waves become just little swells. I turn and see that we're a long way from the shore. Almost a mile! I look around. Water everywhere. Ahead, across the bay it must be two or three miles. It's pretty quiet out here so I relax a little. Tex has his hand shading his eyes, looking for an island or something to sail for. Duane's on his stomach. His hand is dragging in the water. Solid comfort!

The little leaks on the bottom of the boat still trickle and I use my can to bail the water. Everything is under control so we decide to have lunch and plan where we'll head. I'm ready to head home.

The ship floats with the swells as we eat our sandwiches and discuss where we'll go. The sun is now high in the sky so it's getting pretty close to noon.

"Let's go east around the bend to the Rodeo beach." I'm putting in my two cents worth.

Sometimes when Dad isn't working on Sunday, we go to the Rodeo beach and catch sand crabs. It's fun. More important, it's just around the bend, about a mile from where we're now drifting. And we don't have to sail any farther from shore. I wouldn't even have been this brave if I'd known what was happening at this very moment to our "patches" and "putty" job on the hull. The "gentle" constant movement of water across the hull is taking its toll. Ignorance is bliss.

Duane is looking across the bay at the opposite shore. You can just make out the houses along the shoreline and the cars traveling along the side hill road. We can see some real ships that are docked at the Mare Island Shipyard. "Let's go straight across the bay and look at the ships. Maybe they'll even let us climb aboard."

Boy, when Duane gets going there's no stopping him. A motor launch passes about a mile out in the bay. We wave and holler. They don't see us.

Tex has been thinking while Duane and I look at the far shore. He's a pirate and wants to discover a buried treasure. Maybe discover a secret island! Sure enough, we're out in the bay far enough that he can see Alcatraz Island. I know it's about twenty miles from where we live, but out here it looks much closer than Duane's destination across the bay. It's Tex, "Let's sail west for that island. The current will probably help and we should make land in less than an hour. I'll bet we can find all kinds of neat things there."

Tex doesn't know it's a prison. I want no part of it. Even Duane is a bit skeptical. "I don't know, Tex. I think that's a prison and they don't let visitors in at all." Finally, some sense from my "shipmate".

Doesn't phase Tex. We've finished lunch and he's raring to go. "That's even better. I'll bet the beaches on that island haven't been searched for years. No telling what we'll find there."

The idea of finding treasure appeals to Tex. I'm not impressed. I'm getting scared. "Why don't you guys just take me back to shore and I'll wait for you there". Water still isn't my friend, and we're really in water now.

"Boomie, who'd we have to bail if we start taking water? Duane and I have to paddle so you're our baler. We need the full crew to make this a successful trip. It'll only take a couple of hours and we'll be back with our treasures." Tex has spoken. That's the trouble with admiring your uncle. There's no backing down. We're off. Duane on his "stick paddle" and Tex with his "shovel oar!"

I'm bailing. In fact, I seem to be bailing a lot more steadily. I see why. Water is beginning to seep in from the front of the ship where we repaired that board that was sticking way out. The putty seam has disappeared.

"Hey guys, we're taking a lot of water up front." It all flows back to where I'm bailing from the center of the ship.

It's Tex. "Boomie, why not get some putty from the can and see if you can fill the crack again." He's paddling furiously. So is Duane. I grab the putty can and carefully edge my way to the front. As I begin my job, I notice that we're moving along pretty fast directly into the sun that has now dropped from high noon to a much lower position in the western sky. Time flies when you're having fun. I can see that it's mid-afternoon. But, why are we traveling so fast?

Tex notices our speed, too. "We must be in a current or something. I don't even have to paddle and we sail right along." Tex is just sitting on the back seat using the shovel as a rudder, again. Duane stops paddling. We're still moving at the same speed.

Experienced Pirates Three! The Sacramento River flows down the Delta and into the bay. I know this. We've studied it in California History in school. When the tide begins to go out, like it does every afternoon, and its afternoon now, the current is strong toward the Golden Gate Bridge. We're caught in the current and tide. We couldn't change course if we wanted to.

The current, going either in or out is so strong that no one has ever escaped from Alcatraz. I know that, too.

I stop my puttying long enough to share my thoughts, actually my fear, with Tex and Duane.

I could have predicted Tex's reaction. "Great, we're going to be there quicker than I thought. We just have to steer and we'll be landing in a few minutes." Tex is hanging on to the "rudder".

Duane's quiet. We're close enough now that we can see that there aren't any beaches on Alcatraz Island. There are just cliffs of rock hanging for twenty to fifty feet from the water. Now Duane's worried. He sees the sun moving lower into the western sky. I remember that sometimes Dad gets off early on Sunday. Now I'm really worried.

There's a squeak in my voice as I say, "Tex, we'd better change plans. We'll never make it to the island and back to shore in time to get home before Dad. And you know what that will mean!"

Before Tex can respond there's a gush of water and I feel a stream running down my pant leg. I shout, "We've sprung a leak! A big one!"

One of the boards covering a gaping hole has come loose and is hanging by a single nail. Water is shooting into the ship. "Bail!" It's Tex. He's got one can. Duane grabs the other and they begin bailing as fast as they can. I reach for the loose board and try to hold it over the hole. It slows the water down but it's still coming in faster than we can bail. Our ship is gradually filling with water.

We're going to sink and I'm praying, "Oh God, Oh God!".

CHAPTER 6 – LOST AT SEA

Inch by inch the water rises inside our ship as Tex and Duane bail feverishly. The lower we sink the faster the water comes in. It seems like only a minute and the water in our ship is about the same level as the water outside.

"We're goners! We're sinking!" I'm now lying down holding onto the side of the ship. Tex and Duane have stopped bailing and are hanging on too.

It's Tex! "Let's get out of here and hold onto the outside. It's too heavy with us here. The ship's wood and will float if we get out. Just hold onto the side."

Duane slips over the side and holds on. Tex does the same. I'm not leaving. The ship's now almost under water with me right on top.

Then I feel Tex's arm pulling on me. "You've got to get out so the ship won't sink. Hold on to me!"

The top of our ship is now floating right at the waterline. I'm holding onto Tex with one hand and the ship with the other. Duane's on the other side, holding on. We're still moving with the current.

Duane is facing southeast, the direction from which we came. "We're almost in the middle of the bay. Looks like a couple of miles to the shore, either way."

Maybe Duane and Tex think they can swim to shore but they both know I can't make it. I'm not going to cry, but I can feel the 'heaves' in my stomach and chest. I've never been so scared.

Well, maybe once, but not for myself.

It was last summer. Duane and I had been at Grandpa and Grandma's farm all summer. One more week and we had to return home – the end of our adventures with Tex.

We helped Grandpa and Uncle Dee do the haying. Grandpa has about forty acres of alfalfa that is harvested three times during the summer for winter food for his dairy cows. After it's cut and dried, we haul it in the wagon with the horses, into the barn where it is stacked from the bottom to the top. God, it's hot in their pitching the hay under that aluminum roof on the barn.

Well, when we've finished the haying, Tex gets this idea that we can build our own city inside the barn by digging out "roadways" that take us to secret places under the hay. Now the barn is full of hay, right to the roof. We begin our adventure.

It's easy when we start. We all begin digging hay out in front of the cow stanchions. They continue digging and I carry it up to the top of the barn on the ladder that's set up so the cows can be fed their hay from the top. Pretty soon Tex and Duane are several feet under the hay and I can't keep up, going in to get the hay and taking it all the way to the top.

They decide that Tex will dig the hay out to make the tunnels. Duane will bring it out to the entrance and I'll take it to the top. Works great. The longer their tunnels get the less I have to do.

By the time we're called for evening chores we have a regular maze of tunnels under the hay with a couple of "rooms" that are big enough for all of us to sit.

The next day, right after morning chores, we begin "building our city" again. In a couple of hours Tex has tunnels snaking all over under the hay. He digs out a big room where we can almost stand up. We've got a real network of "roads" in our city.

It's hot and stuffy under the hay so Tex asks Duane and me to go to the house and get a jug of water, and maybe Grandma will have some cookies or something for us. We go.

Sure enough, Grandma not only gives us a jug of water but a jug of fresh buttermilk and a bunch of freshly baked cookies. Duane and I really love it here on the farm where everything is so different. We walk across the yard and through the corral to the barn with our

37

stuff. All the way we're talking about how we're going to build more roads in our "under hay" city.

While we've been gone Tex has been digging hay, making our "great room" bigger and piling the hay at the entrance to our city. It's our only entrance.

Duane and I decide to move the hay up the ladder to the top of the barn before going back through the maze to our city. We pick up a couple of arms full of hay that cover the entrance. There's more hay covering the entrance. We decide to dig all the hay out before taking it up the ladder.

The more we dig the more hay that seems to be in the way. We start digging furiously. In just a couple of minutes we realize that the tunnels have collapsed. It's like we're starting from the beginning. Hay everywhere.

Tex is trapped inside!

We keep digging but don't make much progress. It took us several hours to dig the original tunnels. Tex is going to run out of air. He may be squashed, flat.

Now we're scared! This whole adventure is new to both of us. We don't have an idea how long Tex will last under the hay without air coming in the tunnel. We don't know if the hay has crushed him. We're not going to be heroes!

At the same time, we both jump up and run for the house. Grandpa is with Grandma having lunch. I guess we don't make much sense but Grandpa can see that we're scared and something has happened. He keeps asking, "Where's Tex?" We keep saying, "Under the hay."

Finally, Grandpa says, "Show me!"

We're out of there like a shot for the barn. Grandpa is actually jogging behind us. We know what this means. No matter what happens, we're going to feel Grandpa's belt; and it can really be wicked. But we don't care. We're already scared out of our boots.

Finally, at the barn Grandpa can see what we've been talking about. He's got a full vocabulary of four-letter words. He uses all of them as he goes for a pitchfork. Grandma arrives right behind us. She grabs a pitchfork, too. My brother and I stand like a couple of idiots, watching. Grandpa and Grandma are digging hay out as fast as they can. Grandpa's shirt is wet with sweat. Grandma is working and crying. Grandpa just keeps sweating, swearing and working.

It's amazing how much hay Grandpa and Grandma dig out in just a few minutes. Hay everywhere.

It's now been almost an hour since we discovered the "cave in". Even with his strength and endurance we can see that Grandpa is getting really tired. Grandma digs and rests, digs and rests. The air is filled with hay dust and blue with Grandpa's cuss words. He's really mad. And Scared!

I hear a noise as the barn door at the far end cracks open; then opens completely.

There's Tex! He's totally relaxed and strolls toward us. At that same moment Grandpa and Grandma see him. Grandpa really lets out a string of cuss words. Grandma, who is quite heavy, runs like a sprinter, hugging Tex from every angle.

What none of us knew is that the "great room" that Tex had dug out was right up against the barn doors at the north end of the barn. When he'd discovered that the entrance had collapsed and blocked our entrance or exit, he'd just gone back and dug the remaining hay out between the great room and the barn door – and walked out.

I guess we were really lucky that Grandpa was so scared. He even gave Tex a hug, something he never did. He was really relieved. He just told us not to dig into the haystack again and went back to his lunch.

Whew! All three of us have seen "Grandpa's belt" for a lot less. I guess Grandpa had never been so scared. I know I hadn't.

We'd really "messed up" but didn't get the belt. That's the first time I realized that if you "mess up" badly enough, the punishment might be forgiven.

I can feel the current dragging us further and further into the bay. We can see the Golden Gate Bridge way off to the west. A month ago, when we crossed it in the car it was awesome. Even with the setting sun behind it, right now it looks scary. There's a big ship coming under it into the bay.

Duane is holding on to our ship with one hand and paddling with the other. We're not getting any closer to land. Alcatraz Island is the closest. Tex is still holding my arm with one hand and the ship with the other. We can barely see the top of our ship, which is now a couple of inches under water.

It's Tex. "This damn thing is waterlogged. The longer it's under water the more it's going to sink. We're going to have to swim for it Boomie. Duane and I'll stay right next to you and help you swim."

Now I'm terrified. A long swim for me, actually a dog paddle, has been across the pool at the Richmond natatorium. There's no way I'm going to let go of our ship as long as I can hold on.

Duane is still paddling. "Hey, if we all hold on to the side of the ship and kick our feet and paddle we might make it to Alcatraz." He's serious. It's got to be over a mile and we're losing our sinking ship.

CHAPTER 7 – RESCUED: FRIEND OR FOE

We've all been so frantic trying to figure out what to do that we've been blind to what's happening around us. It's Sunday afternoon on the San Francisco Bay. While Tex and Duane are shouting at each other, trying to decide on our best action, I look west again toward the Golden Gate Bridge, the direction the current is taking us. There are dozens of little white sails. People! Lots of them! The Sunday afternoon, informal regatta! It happens every Sunday on the bay, winter and summer.

And one of the sails is coming right at us, maybe a hundred feet away. I almost jump out of my skin as I begin to shout. The same instant Tex and Duane see what I've seen. They both begin shouting at the top of their lungs, also. Duane's arms are flailing in the air.

I can see the sail dropping as the ship comes closer. Nothing has ever looked so beautiful to me. We've just lost our ship, our food and Dad's tools – and I don't care. I thought I was a dead goner. I think Duane and Tex are as relieved as I when they see the arm reaching over the side to help us aboard.

The questions and answers that follow are too crazy for the man, about Dad's age, and his wife to believe. They are out for their regular Sunday cruise around the bay and decide to sail toward the Delta for dinner at a favorite spot. Most of the sailboats cruise the bay between Tiberon and San Jose where the currents aren't strong and the westerly winds make navigation easier. Not many sailboats go east up the river. They have been on a leisurely tack with the wind in their sail and against the current when the wife spots us right in front of them. They'd almost run over us.

When Tex finishes explaining, somewhat dramatically, how we happened to be in the mess they found us in, we are met with silent disbelief. The evidence of what we've done is on our side, so our rescuers, after more talk, begin to believe our story.

Now, safe on a seaworthy sailboat, we, ourselves, have to face the reality of what we've done and the mess we are now in. It's no longer "life or death". It's "Dad's belt"! Not just for what went wrong, but defying his orders to stay out of deep water and most of all losing his tools. We're safe, but really in "deep do do"!

Tex addresses the "skipper". "Hey, since you guys are going upstream anyway, why not just drop us off in Pinole where the creek runs into the bay?" He's trying to talk the "skipper" into taking us back to the beach in Pinole where we launched our ship. At least that way we can walk home.

Just our luck! The "skipper" is a volunteer fireman at the Richmond fire department, He feels responsible to see that we get home safely.

Since rescuing us and hearing our story and, as skipper of his ship, he's in charge. He makes that very clear. "I'll just radio the Harbor Patrol and they'll be here in a few minutes to take you to shore." He's on his radio, talking.

Oh crap! I know what this means. I plead. "If you can just take us over close to shore, we'll be able to make it home okay." We definitely don't want any "assistance" getting home.

That's happened before. I remember like it was yesterday.

We live in Richmond, where I was born. I'm in kindergarten at a school just two blocks from our house. Duane is in the third grade. He and I are about the same size. He'd been sick a lot and the doctors are trying to find out what is going on. Doctors cost money. Dad doesn't like that. Dad works really hard, sometimes on weekends, too, to make extra money. He really wants to have some money in the bank but something always comes up. He and Mom talk about that a lot. He hates being broke. He even hates his job, but he keeps doing it because he can't find anything better. We're in the middle of the depression. It's always been that way.

Back then we didn't get any allowance. Dad only makes a dollar a day at the Sugar Refinery where he works. If we kids want money to spend, we have to earn it. Mostly we work around the neighborhood, cleaning people's yards and sometimes we borrow a lawn mower and mow some lawns. There aren't many jobs and we don't earn very much spending money. Always broke! We aren't old enough to get a job delivering the Richmond Independent paper. Paperboys make a dime a month for every customer. We both look forward to when we'll be able to be paperboys and make maybe $2.00 or $3.00 per month.

Then one day Duane finds our ideal job. In a newspaper at school, he sees a request for "magazine sales people". Just call the number and they deliver "sample" magazines. Then all we have to do is contact people around the neighborhood, show them the samples and collect the price of a subscription. Then once a month we deliver their magazine to them. We get to keep half the subscription money and give the other half to the people that give us the sample magazines. A subscription costs thirty cents a year so for every subscription we make fifteen cents. Big bucks!

Well, Duane calls from school and arranges to get our "Sample Magazines". He's the "sales person". I'm just going to help. We'll split the money. A couple of days later we've got our stuff and are ready to make our fortune.

The first weekend we go to every house for blocks around where we live. Most people are gone. All those at home have magazines galore. Nobody wants to subscribe to our magazines. Not a one!

We're not discouraged. We have friends in Pinole. It's only seven miles away – up over "Tank Farm Hill" along San Pablo Avenue and then down the other side. Sunday afternoon we start walking to Pinole. We know we'll be able to get some subscriptions.

Well, after we leave Richmond we have to walk along San Pablo Avenue, a two-way, three-lane highway that's pretty busy with traffic. We're almost to the top of Tank Farm Hill when a "black and white" police car stops just ahead of us. We're the only "walkers" along the highway. I guess we look pretty small.

The police officer gets out and asks, "Where do you boys live?

43

Are you lost?" His partner gets out the other side.

I'm trying to remember that at school we've been told that the police are here to help us. They're our friends. They don't look very friendly, standing straight and tall in front of us, blocking our way.

Duane is unfazed. "We live at the bottom of the hill, officer. We're not lost. Just on our way to Pinole to visit friends."

"What is it you're carrying there in that bag?" The second officer is speaking.

I'm standing still, mute – scared. Duane decides to level with the officers. "Well, we're actually going to Pinole to get some subscriptions for our magazines. We have a bunch of friends in Pinole." Actually, we only have about three friends there.

The officer doesn't seem very impressed with his explanation. "Do your parents know what you're doing?"

"Well, they know we're out getting subscriptions for our magazines." My brother is thinking pretty good.

"Do they know you're walking to Pinole?" The officer is persistent.

Hesitantly, "Well, not exactly." Not very convincing.

What happens next is, up till then, my worst nightmare. The officers take each of us by the arm and "help" us into the back seat of their patrol car. I feel like a crook being taken to jail. By now I'm beginning to shake from the thought of what is happening. We know what will happen if these guys actually take us home in the police car.

They do. Next thing we know, two uniformed police are escorting us to our front door – their black and white parked right in front of our house.

Dad answers the door. He and Mom just returned from their weekly grocery shopping. That alone always makes Dad mad. He hates to spend the money. By the time the officer explains where he found us and what we were doing, Dad's piercing gray eyes could have burned a hole through the porch door. I can hear his heavy breathing as we are "handed over" and the police officers leave.

I can't even describe what happened next. In those days Dad had a heavy leather razor strap that he used to sharpen his straight razor before shaving. It had a metal end with a loop to hang it on a hook. It was about two feet long and a couple of inches wide.

My brother gets it first. Pants down, on the butt and legs. The metal end of the strap makes a welt with each stroke. God, I stand there shaking – thinking he is never going to quit. I can see blood oozing out of the welts. I close my eyes and wait. I'm next. Pants down – over and over again. I scream as loud as my lungs will permit. I guess Dad gets tired. He quits on me with only about half the beating he'd given Duane.

Our career as magazine salesmen ended. Not a dime. It is about two weeks before either of us can sit down without pain.

We really didn't learn anything except "don't get caught". We didn't think we'd done anything so wrong. We were just trying to make some money. Oh well, we were kind of used to Dad "losing it".

Now Tex, Duane and I are all faced with the same fate. I almost wished I'd drowned. Dad has been waiting for a chance with Tex, to get back at Grandpa, ever since he beat my brother for that apple cider press thing. And now, we've not only defied his orders to stay away from deep water, we've lost some of his tools. Man, I can't even think what that will mean.

I can see that Tex feels the same way. He remembers what I told him about the "rabbit feed" incident that happened just a couple of weeks ago. That one was a real bummer.

Every afternoon before dinner I am responsible for cutting grass from across the street by the baseball field and feeding it to the rabbits. We raise rabbits for food. We have about fifty or sixty in the hutches in the back yard all the time. Dad says feeding them grass saves us about $5 a month on rabbit pellets.

Well, somehow, this evening at dinner Dad asks, "Son, have you fed the rabbits today?"

It's the beginning of baseball season. After school all of the neighborhood kids get together at the baseball field across the street and we "pick" teams and practice. I usually have my hand scythe with me so I can bring the cut grass back when we're called for dinner. Forgot it today.

"I'll do it right after dinner, Dad". My voice is so shaky it sounds like it's coming from someone else's mouth. I look down, avoiding his eyes. God, those eyes can pierce.

No hesitation! He's up off his chair and grabs both Duane and me by the arm and we're in the basement in seconds. His belt off, my brother is first and then me. This time we didn't have to drop our pants so it wasn't that bad. Anyway, a couple of years ago we vowed we'd never cry again when he beat us. Duane held up okay. It's been tough for me. Sometimes I "whimper" some. It hurts. Not so tonight! I don't make a sound.

Dad let Duane go back and finish dinner. I go out and cut grass and feed the rabbits. Then to bed!

We could never understand it. Didn't matter which of us did it, we both, always got the beating. Always Duane first, then me. Either way, it didn't seem fair.

Anyway, this little episode is still fresh in my mind. Both Duane and I will try most anything to avoid the "strap" again, especially this time with Tex, too. We've got to find a way to escape.

CHAPTER 8 – "FAIL BIG" WHEN YOU FAIL

I look around to see if our "ship" is in sight, anywhere. I'm about ready to get back into the water and try to make it to shore with our sinking ship. It's disappeared, completely. We're gradually tacking toward shore, maybe a couple of hundred yards, now. The "skipper" changes directions and sails parallel with the shoreline. The water gets pretty shallow and there are four or five feet of mud under the water. All the cities around the bay have been dumping sewage into the bay for years. Anyone who swims in or sails on the bay knows about the sludge. The "skipper" doesn't want to get stuck in this stuff.

I can see the Harbor Patrol boat coming our way. Tex is still talking to the "skipper".

"I think we're close enough that we can swim to shore, now." It's Tex, making a "last stand" attempt.

I look toward shore. It looks like miles. If we got through the water to the shoreline, we could sink in the muck and never make it. Drown in sludge.

The "skipper" will have none of Tex's proposition. He feels responsible for us now, as though we are his own kids. I wish we were.

The "skipper" drops anchor as the Harbor Patrol pulls up along the side. He's already explained to them on the radio that he's picked us up from our sinking vessel and we need a ride back to shore.

His wife actually hugs us, like we belong to her, as we climb off their ship and onto the Harbor Patrol ship. No one's ever done that to me, especially after I've done some dumb thing. It does give me a lift. Maybe it won't be so bad, after all.

The sun is behind the Golden Gate Bridge by the time we're aboard the Harbor Patrol ship and sailing for the Richmond Point dock. Man, that's miles from home.

Duane, Tex and I are huddled in the front of the ship, trying to avoid any conversation with the crew. We need to plan. The "Captain" already said that he'd have a crew member drive us home when we land.

Tex is first. "Why don't we just tell the guy who takes us back that we live in a different house, on a different street? Then we can walk home, just like yesterday. Sis expects us to be wet and muddy."

Tex is always thinking. He'd make a great criminal. I'm not so sure. "What about the tools and stuff? We asked Dad to use some of his tools last night. He's sure to ask about them. What do we tell him then?"

God knows I've learned not to lie. First, I know I'll go straight to Hell if I lie. How many times has that been drilled into me in Sunday School? But worse, the last time I tried a "little white lie" – not much, just a tiny bending of the truth, Mom found out and absolutely humiliated me by having me drop my pants at the dinner table where she swatted me on the butt. Didn't hurt – just my feelings. My little sister and brother told everyone in town about it. Had to live with that "lie" and punishment for weeks. Never again! I'll take the belt first.

It's getting dark now. We're still not at the dock. It's going to be very late before we're home. Defied Dad's orders, lost his tools, late for dinner – what else? Sometimes it gets so bad it can't get worse. Just face it. I'm really scared. Tex doesn't look much better. Duane's sitting there, silent.

Finally, Tex says, "Why don't we just tell your Dad and Sis what we did and where we've been? Sorta put us on the 'mercy of the court'? We've been there before."

It's been a long, tough day and Tex is tired. He's grasping for straws.

"What mercy?" I'm thinking. Can't lie. Why not try Tex's idea. About the tools, if Dad doesn't ask, no problem. He may never miss them. If he does ask, then we tell the truth.

"Well, Dad's home from work already, so we don't have many choices." What else can we do? By now I'm ready to just go with the flow.

The ship docks and we're given to a really nice lady crew member for the drive home. She asks a hundred questions. Then she talks a mile a minute about our harrowing experience – what could have happened – how lucky we are – and tons of other things.

She's got a daughter and a son about my age. It's a personal thing for her. We get so involved in the discussions with her that we forget we were going to have our "driver" drop us at another home. All of the sudden we're parked in front of our house in Pinole.

It's late and really dark. We sit in the car for a minute. Then we see my aunt Zella come running out of her house. She's got the door open, pulls Tex out and is hugging him like he just came back from the dead. All the time spewing words about what we've been through.

How does she know?

Then Mom and Dad come out of our house. They look like they're in shock. I've never seen Dad this way. He actually grabs me, gives me a hug; same for Duane, then grabs Tex and gives him a hug. Then he puts his hands on Duane's and my shoulders and just pats us. I almost faint!

Mom, in shock, is crying. Aunt Zella, now holding Tex, is also in shock. Our lady driver is crying. Dad looks totally exhausted – almost limp.

Tex, Duane and I are "eating it up". We know we've somehow gotten on a "winning team". Don't know how, but we're enjoying it.

We stand there, amazed. Mom is the first to gain some control. It seems the Captain of the Harbor Patrol called information in Pinole and, being a small place, the operator knew that aunt Zella and Mom are sisters and that aunt Zella has a phone. We don't.

So she put the Captain through to aunt Zella. He didn't mince words telling aunt Zella how lucky she was to still have a younger brother and her nephews. She got all the details – even maybe more dramatic than it'd been, if that's possible. The Captain told the story in a way that he scared aunt Zella out of her wits before he told her that we were okay.

Well, aunt Zella shared the adventure, in the same way with Mom and Dad. She particularly loved the idea of "getting even" with my dad. His reputation for corporal punishment was well known among Mom's family. I guess she really "laid it on", for Dad was really shook.

Anyway, we're really relieved when we realize we're not going to "get the belt".

"FAIL BIG!"

The lady driver leaves.

Our family has a great dinner that night. The dinner table, for the first time I ever remember, buzzes with conversation. Both Dad and Mom want to know every detail about our last two days, from beginning to end. Dad, by the time we finish dinner, desert and conversation, is absolutely animated as he jokes about the supplies and tools we used for our "ship" and lost at sea.

Yes, we "failed big" this time. In any other situation, there are a dozen reasons we'd get the belt for what we did. I guess the thought of our drowning in the bay really scared everyone, importantly, Dad.

The rest of that week, Tex, Duane and I are famous, among the family and around town.

Easter week ends, and Tex goes back to the farm. School starts – back to reality.

PART TWO: ALFRED AND ME

WHO'S DISABLED?

CHAPTER 9 – PICKING UP THE PIECES

I've lived in Pinole since kindergarten. All my friends live here. I finished the sixth grade this year.

It's September. Mom and I just returned from a month staying with my Uncle Don and Aunt Bean in Potter Valley. My little brother and sister stayed in Pinole with Aunt Zella.

It was supposed to be a vacation. We picked pears for three weeks for one of the farmers in the valley. No playing, no swimming, no friends, no fun. It wasn't that bad though. I made over twenty dollars picking pears, a fortune.

My Uncle Don and his older brother, my Uncle Reed, both bought farms in Potter Valley a few years ago. It was dry farming when they moved in. A few years ago, the Electric Company cut a tunnel through the mountain from the valley to Eel River. The water from Eel River comes through the mountain and operates their power plant at the north end of the valley. Now there's lots of water in the Russian River that runs through the center of the valley. The river divides it into east and west sides.

With all this new water, the farmers got together and formed an irrigation district to use the river water to irrigate their farms. Now they can grow almost anything they want. Mostly they grow alfalfa for hay and they grow clover as pastureland for their dairy cows. The water also irrigates the pear orchards, and grape vineyards.

Actually, this whole year hasn't been much fun. And, Easter vacation wasn't the same, at all. Duane and I tried everything we could think of, but we missed Tex too much to have fun.

Nobody around our house talks about it much. It's been almost a year now. The whole summer vacation from school has been a waste. Hardly any fun like we had in the past.

Duane and I used to spend the summer at Grandpa and Grandma's farm. We always did lots of work on the farm, but also had time for lots of adventures with Tex.

This whole summer, Duane's been in Potter Valley helping Uncle Reed and Uncle Don on their farms. I didn't even know where Potter Valley was – and didn't care. I have to stay here in Pinole with Mom, Dad and my little brother and sister anyway, so I can deliver the paper route. It's really Duane's job but he gave it to me for the summer. I get ten cents a month for every customer. That's nine dollars a month. I feel rich! My allowance from Mom is twenty-five cents twice a month. But even the money doesn't help how I feel.

Grandpa and Grandma don't have the farm anymore. Every time I think about it, it seems like a really bad movie – stuff like this only happens in movies.

It's a Sunday morning in October. I'm eleven and a half years old now. I'm in the Scouts. Alfred, my best friend, is in the scouts with me so we spend a lot of time together. I've known Alfred since kindergarten. We keep busy with projects to earn awards. We're competing against some of our friends to see who can earn the most awards. I think every boy in the sixth grade is a scout.

Anyway, on this Sunday morning Alfred and I are planning an expedition across the hills to El Sobrante so we'll earn a hiking award. We have all our supplies packed and we're sitting on the front porch with the map we've drawn to where we're going. We aren't sure exactly how far it is across the hills, but it has to be shorter than along the highway.

Suddenly I hear Mom's sister, Aunt Zella, who lives just two houses down the block, screaming as she runs toward us. She isn't just crying, more wailing like a wounded animal. A second later she is at our house, tears running down her face, sobs between words I can't make out, running up the porch stairs and in the front door. She hasn't even seen Alfred and me as she stumbles over us. The only thing I hear is "dead, they're both dead".

Alfred has been through a lot but he knows something really bad has happened. He just looks at me, gets up and says, "I'll see you later, Boomie", and he leaves.

I sit alone on the porch for a minute. I've never seen Aunt Zella like this before. I've never even seen her cry. She and my Uncle Fred own a small grocery store here in Pinole and I sometimes deliver groceries to their customers for them. They are always so happy and fun to be around. My Uncle Fred taught me to play tennis. He'll play a set of tennis with me for every game of monopoly I'll play with him. He's a kid at heart and really loves monopoly. He also plays professional baseball, but that's a whole 'nuther story.

Behind me from the house I can hear all sorts of commotion. There's shouting. I can hear crying. My little sister comes out the front door, tears running down her face as she sobs. My stomach is in my throat. I want to just walk away and let whatever is happening, happen, without me. I know it's got to be really terrible.

The last time Aunt Zella came running to our house like this was a Sunday, also! That time we learned that we were at war. Pearl Harbor. Nothing has been the same since. I'm thinking, maybe the Japs are coming. We have air raid drills all the time. All at once I'm scared.

My little sister is only five. Through her sobs she's saying something about them being dead. A train! Finally, it's too much for me. I've got to find out. Up the stairs and into the house!

Dad's at work. Since the war started, he's worked seven days a week in the shipyards. There in the living room is my big brother, Duane, my little brother, Bruce, and Mom with Aunt Zella. Duane and Bruce are just standing there with their hands in their pockets, staring at Mom and Aunt Zella. Mom and Aunt Zella are holding each other, both crying uncontrollably. I feel like leaving. I'm already beginning to cry just from seeing what's happening.

Duane sees me standing by the front door and comes over to me. In our family we don't show much emotion, except when we feel Dad's belt. There's no hugging or kissing and stuff like that. But now, for the first time in my life, Duane puts his arms around me and squeezes me. I'm ready to faint. What can be this terrible? Did something happen to Dad or Uncle Fred?

A couple of months ago my Uncle Ted, home on leave from his Army training, ran his motorcycle into a train. Destroyed the motorcycle but didn't hurt him. Has something happened to Uncle Ted?

Duane pulls me back out on the front porch. His eyes are wet. I can't believe it. Duane never cries. When Dad gives us "the belt" we vowed we'd never cry. I sometimes can't quite make it but not Duane. He's tough. He can see that I'm already terrified.

He whispers, yet like the sound of a cannon, the words ring around in my head and in my ears. The space around me darkens until I can't even see. "Grandma and Uncle Tex were hit by a train and they're both dead!"

I think Duane is in shock. I know I am. Death is not a part of an eleven-year old's world. Not Grandma and Uncle Tex! There's my little sister, sitting on the front porch, now helplessly sobbing. Her body shuddering! Duane steps back. I can see the tears welled up in his eyes. I feel total helplessness envelop my body. I can't cry. I don't believe what I'm hearing or seeing. I can still hear Mom and Aunt Zella crying.

I've got to get away. I run down the stairs, across the baseball field and up the hillside where I fly kites. I keep running till I'm so tired I can't breathe. Everything's changed. I know it can't be true. I know Duane doesn't lie. Mom and Aunt Zella don't cry. Grandma and Tex can't be dead. I kick the grass, throw rocks, break branches off the trees and stomp on them. Finally, I lay down. Nothing is the same.

It's Duane. I feel cold. I guess I fell asleep. The sun's gone. Duane is just sitting next to me, quietly looking, at nothing. He's got his hand on my back. He's been crying. For the first time in my life, I kneel next to him and hug him. He hugs me back. We both sob.

Now I know it's true. Grandma and Uncle Tex are gone. I'll never see them again. I'm so filled with emptiness I can't feel a thing. Duane and I get up and start back to the house.

Gradually I'm overcome with how important my big brother is to me. Thank God, I've got him. We can make it through this. I realize, once again, how much I admire him. We've been through lots together. Now, together, we'll get through this.

With my brother, Duane, in Potter Valley, it was a long summer. Thank God for Alfred. He really helped me, from the start of this year's vacation.

CHAPTER 10 – TREASURE OR TROUBLE

When this year's summer vacation started, I knew I'd be spending a lot of time with Alfred. Usually, I'd be chasing around after Duane and his friends. They're always into some kind of fun. His buddies, Bradley and Buster don't have little brothers, and think I'm a "creep", but Duane stands up for me and lets me "run with them" most of the time. But he's gone to Potter Valley for the summer.

Staying here in Pinole without Duane would have been the total pits except for Alfred. We've been best friends since kindergarten. Next fall we'll start seventh grade together.

And, if it weren't for Alfred's adventuresome spirit – always looking to explore the "wilderness" and the "mountains" around Pinole Valley, my summer might have been terrible.

Actually our "wilderness" is along Pinole Valley Creek that runs from a couple of miles up in the hills down to the bay. And our "mountains" are the wooded hills that border the valley on both sides of Pinole.

One of Alfred's and my goals this summer is to fly a kite clean across the Pinole Valley, from the hill behind my house to the "school on the hill". We almost made it one really windy day during Easter vacation. Would have, too, but the wind tore our kite off the frame.

We'd made the kite twice the size of any we'd ever seen. Wound thread around double pieces of balsa wood to make it big. Then used flour and water paste to attach the wrapping paper to the frame. We found after the kite went down that the "paste" just didn't hold against so much weight and wind. Right then we decided we'd get some real glue and do it again. Before we got the supplies, Easter vacation was gone so our "kite flying goal" had to wait.

Anyway, when school let out, the first week of June, Alfred comes to my house with me. It is noon. We have the whole afternoon.

Walking down the hill from the school with Alfred I ask, "Hey, why don't we go down to Ruffs and look at comic books?" Ruffs is the main store in town. Mr. Ruff doesn't like us handling the new comic books, but since Alfred is his best customer, he doesn't chase us out like he does other kids.

"I've got all the new ones at home. Let's follow the creek out to my place. We can look for stuff in the creek as we go." Alfred loves to explore.

"Let's go. I don't have to be home till the papers arrive." I deliver the Richmond Independent papers every afternoon. They arrive at 5:00 o'clock and I have them delivered within an hour. We used to have family dinner at 6:00 o'clock sharp, but since Dad is working all kinds of overtime at the shipyards, we kind of have dinner when we get home, instead.

We're on our way. By now the creek doesn't have much water, just a trickle. There are lots of little pools with small fish. And, lots of trash and stuff scattered along the banks. We kick cans, check the paper bags and look under rocks and fallen limbs to see it there is any "treasure".

About half mile out of town I spy what looks like a new pile of small rocks up the bank under a bush. It wasn't there, or at least we didn't see it a couple of Saturdays ago when we were here. They're so neatly stacked under the bush we think it may be a grave for an animal. Or, someone may have marked something they've hidden.

"Hey, look at that." I grab Alfred. "Looks funny. Let's see what's under these rocks".

We climb the bank and crawl under the bush. The pile of rocks has some small branches tossed over it.

"Someone did this on purpose, trying to hide something." Alfred is beginning to move rocks to the side.

"Careful. This may be an animal grave. Ugh!" Alfred keeps moving rocks – a little slower.

There are lots of rocks. They fill a hole over a foot deep that's been dug. Finally, we remove the last of the rocks and there it is. We know it is something valuable. A treasure!

It's wrapped in a big rubber bag. The rubber bag is sealed at the top with what looks like a piece of lead holding a waxed cord. When my friend, Robert and I went to see his father at the bank where he worked, we sometimes saw the bags of money sealed this way. Alfred takes the bag from me. He's always ready. Out with his boy scout knife and he has the bag open in a couple of seconds. He takes out two small leather bags. Something's in them! One feels a little oily. He dumps it on the ground. There are two boxes, covered with wax. He reaches in the second leather bag with his hand. We both gasp as he removes the contents.

Alfred speaks first. "We've got to get this out of here. Who knows why it was hidden? It looks brand new."

We look around to make sure no one sees us. It's clear. "Let's take it out to your place. We can check it out and see if it works okay. I know I can't take it home. If my dad found out it would be the belt, really big time." We're both excited; I'm a little scared.

"How do we get it out of here without someone seeing us?" Alfred's right. With school just out there could be lots of other kids in the area. We'd never make it out Valley Road to his place without running into some of them.

I'm beginning to feel like a criminal – sneaking around. "We can't leave it here. Someone else might find it." I'm watching Alfred as he "handles" it.

"Let's take it up the creek to Silva's. They have all that hay stacked in the field next to the creek. We can hide it under a hay stack and pick it up in a day or two when there aren't so many people around." Alfred knows the stacks of hay in the fields at Silva's dairy aren't touched till fall when they start feeding them to the cows.

We each put a bag under our shirt and "sneak" up the creek bed until Silva's dairy is in sight. There's a big haystack just a few feet from the creek bank. In a couple of minutes we've dug a hole about three feet into the hay. We put our treasure in the hole and stuff the hay back in place.

We've been so busy with our treasure we haven't noticed the passing of time. We don't have watches but can see the sun is way past noon.

"Alfred, it's too late to go out to your place now. I'll be late with my papers. Let's leave everything like it is and we'll come back after the baseball game tomorrow."

We cross the field. Alfred goes out Valley Road toward home. I go the other way, to downtown Pinole, to get my papers.

Our secret treasure is safe.

CHAPTER 11 – BUCK THE COP AND ALFRED

The San Pablo Highway connects Pinole with other towns west of San Francisco. It doubles as Pinole's main street. Buck, the Cop, sits on his motorcycle on Valley Road, the side street at the bottom of the hill leading into town. Buck is always ready to catch drivers who speed through town. Buck is busy every day. Almost everyone who doesn't live here ends up speeding down the hill that runs through town and they get to meet Buck.

Because of Buck, Pinole is famous. It's his personal "speed trap". I guess everyone in town is happy with the money from Buck's speeding tickets. None of the people who live here complain about him.

The truck delivers my papers right next to where Buck parks.

Sometimes on quiet days Alfred and I sit under the shade of the trees that line Valley Road where Buck parks his motorcycle, watching and counting each time Buck roars away after another speeder; his red lights flashing and siren blasting.

We dream about being cops. Buck looks like a space ranger in his tan uniform, tight jacket, captain's hat and leather boots laced almost to his knees. Each time he comes back to his hiding place Alfred and I stand and salute. He always tips his hat as he backs his motorcycle into position, ready for the next speeder.

Sometimes he lets one of us sit on the bike with him while he waits and watches. When a speeder passes, we jump off as Buck stands to kick the pedal that starts his bike. While Buck is gone, Alfred and I talk about how exciting it'll be when we're cops and chase speeding motorists. We'll always have our pistols ready when we stop a car. Neither Alfred nor I have ever fired a pistol, but we know exactly what we'll do when we have one.

That's why Alfred and I are so excited now. A couple of times Buck has shown us his pistol. Even let us hold it – after he'd removed the bullets. Since the war started most of the kids have "guns". Some of them look pretty real, but they're actually made of wood or rubber. Alfred and I both have "rubber" rifles and pistols.

As I sit rolling my papers today, I'm so excited I can barely get the rubber bands around them. My mind is going a hundred miles an hour. I've got visions more real than I've ever had.

Now, Alfred and I are actually going to have our own, real pistol.

Tomorrow we'll dig our "treasure", the pistol, from the hay pile. And we have two boxes of bullets, too.

I watch Buck, sitting there, his pistol in his leather holster. I feel my hand reaching down by my side, pressing against my own holster. Suddenly Buck is gone. I've got to get my papers ready.

I keep rolling papers. Can't quit thinking! A brand-new pistol, a revolver, with lots of bullets! I'm not sure if I'm happy, excited or just plain scared about having a real gun. I don't know what Alfred's dad will do when he finds out, but I know what would happen to me. Dad would kill me, not with the gun, with his belt. With Duane gone for the summer I'll get the whole beating, alone. I decide it's worth it. Dad probably won't find out, anyway. We'll just practice with it up in the woods, behind Alfred's place. No houses near and lots of trees. No problem!

Alfred and I are almost exactly the same age. We're the same size. He's got curly red hair and so many freckles he looks like he's got a suntan all year. I hardly notice it, but he has only one arm.

Years ago, when he was just four years old, Alfred's dad took him for a ride on his new Harley motorcycle. Their ride together was a way for them to get away from their grief. Just the day before the whole town was at the funeral for Alfred's mom. A few days earlier she'd been killed when a train crushed her inside her car as she crossed the railroad tracks on the way to Hercules to visit a friend. It was the same place my Uncle Ted ran into the train.

Alfred's dad bought the motorcycle about a month before and was just learning to ride it. Seems kinda crazy that his mom didn't want his dad to buy the bike. Too dangerous! Then she gets killed in her car. I'm learning; life ain't always fair.

Alfred and his dad were taking their first ride together. They'd been out riding all over town for about half an hour. While cruising down Valley Road toward their house, about a mile south of town, they hit the gravel driveway at Silva's dairy. The motorcycle lost traction and flopped. I've done that on my bike a dozen times when Mom sent me out to get the gallon of milk, we buy every couple of days from Silva's.

Alfred's dad jumped clear as the motorcycle fell and skidded on the loose gravel, jamming against a fence post. Alfred got caught under the rear wheel. His left arm got stuck between the wheel sprocket and the chain. The sprocket and wheel were going around about a hundred miles an hour.

His dad jumped up and ran to the bike. It was too late. By the time he was able to shut the motor off Alfred's left arm was gone. Holding him in one arm, Alfred's dad tore up the road on his motorcycle, rushing Alfred to the doctor's office in Rodeo, two miles away. He was really bleeding.

He got blood and they said he was in shock. But it was too late for his arm. They had to amputate it just below the elbow, leaving Alfred with his upper left arm and a two-inch stub below his left elbow.

The accident devastated Alfred's dad. He was really broken. He'd lost his wife and now he felt responsible for what happened to Alfred.

From that day on, he couldn't do enough for his only son. Yet, the only difference I ever saw between Alfred and all the rest of us was that he had his dad's permission to buy every comic book that was printed. And, starting in the third grade, he did.

That's one of the reasons I like to spend so much time with Alfred. He buys every new comic book as soon as it comes out. His attic room is like a library of comic books. Until I got Duane's paper route, I could only afford to buy maybe one or two comic books a year.

Most of the time when Alfred and I aren't in town dreaming of being cops, we're with Flash Gordon and Buck Rogers in worlds all around the galaxy. We are the first star travelers; the first aliens on foreign planets; the conquerors of new worlds throughout the universe. Our star ship is a two-sectioned orange crate. Alfred and I take turns being the pilot in the front seat or the navigator in the back.

Finally, my papers are rolled and I'm ready to deliver. Tomorrow will arrive soon enough.

CHAPTER 12 – A LESSON LEARNED

I always hate to miss a day of school. It's not that I liked going to school that much. I just don't want to miss anything the teacher says. Like it will leave a hole in my life that I'll never be able to fill. And I really don't want one of the "smart" girls to get ahead of me. I'd fake being well when I was sick so as not to miss a day of school.

It all started in the first grade.

On the first day of school, after Christmas vacation, Mrs. Collins, our teacher, announced a reading contest. We'd learned to read kid books in kindergarten last year and first grade started with lots of time spent on reading. The pupil that read the most books during the next month of school would receive a prize. If a girl won, she'd get a doll. If a boy won, he'd get a baseball glove. To show that we'd read the books we had to hand in a "book report" on a 3x5 card.

I knew that first day that the baseball glove was mine. All I had for a baseball glove was a beat up "rag" given to me by my Uncle Fred, after he'd worn it out. This was my first school competition, especially with girls. I decided I'd read at least a book a day – and I did – in fact when the month ended, I'd read over fifty books (it's the first grade – they're small) and turned in over fifty book reports. I'd won the contest by over twenty books.

I accepted my new baseball glove. Man was I excited. I was proud that I'd beaten the girls but I was really excited about the new glove.

I figured that if I hadn't been at school that day, I'd have been late to learn of the reading competition and wouldn't have won the baseball glove.

Anyway, this summer I discovered that sometimes there's a lot more to be learned from experience than from the classroom. I know Alfred agrees with me.

Saturday, our first full day of summer vacation! Our buddies and we are going to play a baseball game against the Rodeo team. It's the first game of the summer. We don't have coaches or uniforms. A bunch of kids in each nearby town or school get together and form a team. Today we play Rodeo. Rodeo is two miles away. Their team will walk and bike to Pinole where we're playing the game.

In Pinole, baseball is the game of choice. In fact, it's not really a choice. It's the only game we play at school. The School on the Hill where we go has an asphalt baseball diamond for each grade from the first to the sixth. Then for the seventh and eighth graders there is a dirt and grass field on a dug out flat area just below the school. Baseball is played at every recess, lunch hour and after school. No coaches! The school has nine lady teachers, one for each grade from kindergarten to eighth, and a janitor, the only man.

Alfred and I have been playing baseball since the first grade. He can wrap his left elbow stump around the bat and swing as hard as any of us. And in the field he uses a left handed glove on his right hand, catches the ball, tosses the glove and ball into the air, catches the ball with his right hand and throws it, all just as fast as most of us who have two working arms and hands. I guess that's why I've never really thought of Alfred as being disabled in any way. There's nothing that I do that he doesn't do at least as well.

He even plays tennis. I live on Plum Street, across from the fire station and the town's two tennis courts. Tennis isn't very popular, so the courts are almost always empty when any of us kids want to play. Uncle Fred taught Duane to play right after we moved to Plum Street. Later, Duane and uncle Fred taught me to play. I taught Alfred and then we became "real tennis players" together, playing almost as much tennis as we did baseball. Then we taught some of our friends to play.

So, it is kind of natural that Alfred and I play lots of tennis. He nuzzles the tennis ball into the bend of his stumped left elbow, tosses it up and serves it as well as anyone. I win a few more sets than Alfred because I've played tennis with Duane and uncle Fred, but the wins come only after he makes me really work for them.

Anyway, this morning Alfred is at my house before 8:00 o'clock. We're going to beat the Rodeo baseball team and then go back out to the Silva farm and claim our treasure.

Usually, we're really excited about a baseball game but today we can't think of anything but our new pistol, hidden in the hay.

The ball game's over a little before noon and we're ready to go. Rodeo really "creamed" our team, but we don't even care. We've got more important stuff today.

Mom has tuna sandwiches ready for us when we arrive home, across the street from the baseball field.

"What are you boys going to be doing today?" Mom knows Alfred and I will be going somewhere.

We haven't discussed our "treasure" yet, so I speak up before Alfred can "spill the beans". "We're going out to Alfred's place. He has all the new comic books so we're going to read for a while. Then we'll probably hike up the hill and maybe fly our kites."

I look at Alfred. He has a questioning look on his face. Mouth full of sandwich, he speaks, "Yes, Mrs. Foster, we're going to be really busy this afternoon. You wouldn't believe what we have planned."

Mom responds. "Oh, I think I might. Just try me."

Alfred's about to do it! No fear! With his Dad he can do just about anything. I don't think he's ever "felt the belt". I almost bark, "It's really nothing, Mom. It's our first full day of vacation. We'll probably do some exploring along the creek on the way out to Alfred's place. You know all the stuff we find along the creek bed."

"Just you boys stay out of trouble. And, be sure you remember your papers this afternoon."

Whew! We're out of there. Alfred has half his sandwich in his hand and I'm dragging him by his stump.

"Man, we've got to keep our gun a secret. If my Dad ever finds out he'd beat the crap out of me and ground me for the summer."

Alfred looks surprised. No one knows about the "rules" my dad sets down and what happens if Duane or I "bend" or break one. Even Alfred doesn't know. It's something Duane and I don't talk about much. "Hey, I know we don't want the other kids to know about our find, but I thought it was okay to tell family. I know it's okay with my dad."

"Alfred, friend, let's just keep it our secret for a while. Nobody needs to know. We don't even know who hid the pistol. It could be a murder weapon. Or maybe someone robbed a bank with it. I'll watch the papers to see if anyone reports anything. Maybe in a few days we'll know. Okay?" I don't mention the real reason I want to keep it a secret.

We're on our bikes and almost to Silva's farm, our backpacks in place. There are haystacks all around the field. Coming in from the road we're not sure which is the one where we hid our treasure. We park our bikes at the edge of the field and walk across to the creek. Now we see the haystack.

Minutes later we have the pistol and ammunition in our packs and we're on our way to Alfred's. With our treasure now in our possession we're both too excited to even talk.

Alfred's dad is at home, working in his yard. He has a huge yard, maybe a couple of acres. He raises lots of vegetables. He even has some apple, peach and pear trees.

From the porch Alfred shouts, "Hi Dad. Boomie and I are going to spend some time in the attic reading comics."

"You guys know there's a Three A baseball game this afternoon in Hercules. Your Uncle Fred's playing, isn't he Boomie?" Alfred's dad loves baseball. The team my Uncle Fred plays for, Three Brother's Service, is a kinda farm team for the Oakland Oaks.

"He signed up as a reserve for the Navy or Marines the first of the year. Last week they called him and he's on a ship, somewhere. Aunt Zella is really 'ticked'. She didn't even know he'd volunteered."

"Well, the war is affecting a lot of us." Alfred's dad is about my dad's age. They say they're too old and won't have to go into the Army.

It's Alfred. "Dad, we're going to pass on the ball game today. We played this morning. Got trounced! We'll probably be here when you get back."

We're in the attic sitting on Alfred's bed. The pistol and the two boxes of bullets are between us. We hear Alfred's dad leave in his car. We're alone.

Alfred is studying the writing on the pistol. "It's a Smith and Wesson, Model 38, whatever that means." Neither Alfred nor I actually know anything about real guns. My dad has a huge shotgun that I've seen. He keeps it in his bedroom in the closet. We're not allowed in there so I've never really looked at it. There are no guns in Alfred's house. Since the war began lots of people have talked about buying all kinds of guns and stuff to protect themselves in case of an invasion. Some people may have, but not in Alfred's or my house.

I'm counting the bullets. There are 30 in each box. They feel kinda oily. A little comes off on my hands. "Let's see how the bullets go in the gun." I'm anxious to go out back into the woods and try to shoot a tree or something.

Alfred is working with it. There's a cylinder that pops out when a small lever is pushed. He's got it open. "It holds six bullets." Alfred takes six bullets and puts them into the cylinder. He closes it. The cylinder snaps into place. "I think it's ready to shoot." Alfred is aiming it at the ceiling. "The trigger won't move. It's stuck."

"Hey, don't pull the trigger in here. We'll put a hole through the roof." I'm somewhere between excited and scared.

"No problem. The trigger won't even move. Something's holding it." Alfred's got the pistol between his legs checking everything. He

68

moves the little lever and the cylinder pops out. He puts it back. Then he pulls the hammer back. There's a click.

We don't know it but pulling the hammer back releases the safety. He pulls on the trigger again.

CRACK! It sounds like a cannon went off in the attic. The pistol jumps in Alfred's hand. There's a hole in the floor right next to his foot.

"WOW!" That was close." We kneel down and look at the hole in the floor. We can see right through to the kitchen below.

We drop the pistol on the bed and run downstairs to the kitchen. There in the floor, in the corner of the kitchen is a small, round hole with the bullet sticking up. I look out the window to see if anyone heard the shot. Nothing unusual! Alfred has the bullet out of the floor. He says, "Hardly noticeable."

I look up. "Yeah, but there's a hole in the ceiling. What are we going to do about that?"

Out the door and back in a flash, Alfred has a small can of putty and a putty knife. Good scouts. Be prepared. In just a couple of minutes we've got the hole in the ceiling filled with putty. It almost vanishes.

"How often do we look at the ceiling, anyway?" Alfred's satisfied. He returns the putty to the garage. We're back on the bed with our now "dangerous weapon".

"Okay, one close call is enough. Let's take the bullets out of the pistol till we figure out how it works." I'm not so sure our pistol is such a "treasure", now. Some excitement is okay but this is a bit much. I've been caught doing less and "felt the belt" too many times.

Alfred takes the bullets out of the pistol and puts them in his pocket. I take the pistol and inspect it. There's a little "button" above the trigger guard that moves. Push it one way and the trigger locks. Push it the other and it releases the trigger. We both test it. Pull the hammer back and the button always releases the trigger. We're beginning to understand how the pistol works. We both try it several times, pulling the trigger and listening to the "snap" as it releases into an empty cylinder.

Alfred locates one of his "play gun holsters" and puts it on. The pistol fits, loosely. He quick draws! Again and again!

I put the holster on and practice. We're getting pretty good and confident.

I put on another of Alfred's holsters. I grab a cap pistol and a couple of rolls of caps. Alfred has the 38.

We're ready to explore the hills behind Alfred's house.

CHAPTER 13 – WHOOPS!

There are miles of woods behind Alfred's house out in the Pinole Valley. And, there's lots of brush in between all the trees. Over the last three years Alfred and I have explored these hills all the way to El Sobrante, cutting some of the thick brush away to create trails.

Last year, about a half-mile from his house we built a fort in a big oak tree out of dead branches we collected. Then we cut a ladder right up the trunk of the tree so we can climb up to our fort.

Sometimes we're with Tarzan, deep in the forest of Africa, hunting elephants and lions. We have a rope tied to a limb that lets us escape fast by swinging down to the ground The first one coils the rope and throws it to the second, who follows. We've hit the ground pretty hard a few times when we didn't take enough slack out of the rope before jumping.

"Let's go to the fort and search for wild game. No one will hear us way out there." Alfred leads the way up the hill.

It only takes about ten minutes to get to our fort. We climb up the trunk to the platform we've built. From here, through the trees, we can see both ways up and down the Pinole Valley Road. There are some cans and bottles under our fort. We sometimes raid Alfred's kitchen and bring cans of food and bottles of soft drinks – for when we're going to take a long hike.

Spotting the "targets", Alfred climbs down and "sets them up" on a hanging branch of a nearby tree – about twenty-five feet from my position in the fort. "Let's have some target practice." Alfred's back, pistol in hand. It seems so quiet. He loads the pistol.

There are six bottles and two cans, our "targets" perched on the tree limb. Alfred hands me the pistol. "You take the first shot. You found the pistol".

We've seen tons of movies, particularly Westerns, with cowboys shooting pistols all over the place. And we've seen some "cop and robber" movies, where the pistol is held in both hands by the cops when they meet up with the crooks.

"How should I hold this thing?" I extend my right arm and try to aim down the barrel. "It feels kind of wobbly." I try holding it in both hands. Still wobbly! And Alfred has only one hand. I decide on "Western" style and point the pistol at the closest bottle with my right hand. I pull the trigger. Nothing!

"You gotta release the safety, Boomie, remember?" I'd completely forgotten the safety that locks the trigger.

"Okay, got it". I release the safety and, in a kneeling position stretch my right arm toward the bottle, pistol in my hand, ready for my first shot. "**CRACK!**" Even outside it sounds like a cannon went off in my ear. I quickly looked around to see if anyone could have heard the shot. "WOW! This thing is loud!"

Alfred ignores the noise. He's down by the branch with our "targets". They are all still perched on the branch. "You missed. But pretty close! The slug's here in the bark." Alfred is peeling bark from the branch where there's a small hole.

He comes back and we sit on the floor. Alfred takes the pistol, sits with his knees raised and rests his elbow on his knee as he takes aim. "**CRACK!**" Another cannon shot. But this time the sound of breaking glass as a bottle disappears from the tree limb.

"Great shot! You hit a bottle, dead on." I'm excited. Before I can say anything else there's another "**CRACK**" and a second bottle disappears.

Alfred hands the pistol back to me. "Why don't you try sitting and putting your arm on your leg. It's easy." We're really getting into this, now. In fact, we're concentrating on what we're doing so much we don't hear or notice that we have company.

There's a loud "A-HEM" right below us. I'm sitting with the pistol, ready to fire. Alfred is sitting next to me, watching. We both turn.

There's Alfred's dad. That's not bad. Next to him, in his uniform, is the sheriff, who just happens to be a friend of Alfred's dad.

The sheriff speaks – actually yells, "What do you boys think you're doing up there? This place sounds like a combat zone."

Alfred's dad is frowning, but he doesn't look really mad, like I've seen my dad. "Where'd you boys get the pistol?" I think Alfred's dad is just curious.

It turns out, the baseball game was canceled because of a scheduled air raid warning test. Alfred's dad invited the sheriff home with him for a couple of beers. What luck!

My mouth is dry. I can't talk. Alfred takes the pistol from my hand, sets it down, and looks his dad right in the eye. "We found the pistol yesterday, Dad! We thought this would be a safe place to try it out." Matter of fact truth! That's Alfred.

Alfred's dad gives a questioning look at the sheriff. The sheriff is silent. "Okay boys. You'd better come down now. No harm done. We'll talk about the pistol back at the house."

Whew! I almost peed my pants.

Back at Alfred's house, between Alfred's dad and the sheriff, we have a real lesson in "firearms". Things I'll never forget. And I haven't.

How to make sure the chamber is empty. How to be sure the safety is on and working. How to properly load the cylinder. Keeping the pistol clean. And, never point a loaded or empty pistol at anyone.

Later in the afternoon the sheriff takes all of us back to our fort and shows us how to become "marksmen" with the pistol. He demonstrates how to hold it in two hands with one elbow resting against the chest to steady the hands. He shows Alfred how to use his left elbow the same way to steady the pistol in his right hand. We can actually hit the bottles from about 20 feet.

This goes on for a couple of hours. Everyone practices. By the end of the afternoon, we use all of the bullets we'd found.

I think that was the sheriff's plan.

We stand quietly by as the sheriff gets Alfred's dad to assure him that any further practice with the pistol will be with his supervision. Alfred's dad says he'll take control of the pistol and there'll not be a further problem.

I had to really speed out of there on my bike back into town to get my papers rolled and delivered.

And Alfred's dad meant it about our pistol. That was the last I saw of it for the rest of the summer.

CHAPTER 14 – SURPRISE! SURPRISE!

Mrs. Jordan, the seventh-grade teacher is tall, with black hair and a scowl on her face. Duane warned me about her. She's tough!

The first day of school! I always like it. There's no homework, no books yet and all we do is listen to the teacher tell us the things we're going to study and learn this year. And long recesses with baseball games!

Like a giant, standing at the front, center of the classroom, Mrs. Jordan speaks. "There's no time to waste. Let's find out what you know."

She has a seating chart in her hand. For the next hour she's asking questions; drilling us about stuff we were supposed to have learned last year but mostly forgot over the summer. She'd call a student by name and then fire a question. Everybody was trying to hide by squatting low in their desks. Hardly anyone answered a question the way she wanted. She'd tell them what's wrong with their answer but not what is right.

After grilling all of us, finally she said, "Okay, I guess you know it's not going to be a picnic in seventh grade this year. We've got to get you prepared for high school and there's not much time. Open your desks and you'll find your textbooks for the year. In each book is your daily assignment. Your homework is due at the beginning of each period. No excuses! We'll have an oral quiz every day. You're excused from school for the rest of the day. Be on time in the morning, complete your homework and be prepared for the quiz."

None of us knew whether to laugh or cry. Only one hour of school today! But homework, already?

Duane didn't exaggerate. I really like learning. I'm not sure I like it this much. Alfred and I join the guys on the school ground baseball field for a game before going home and beginning the real schoolwork. We like to study together so we decide on my place.

We know from our experience that my little brother and sister will still be in their classes until later in the afternoon so we'll have some privacy.

When we reach my house Alfred speaks. "Isn't that your dad's car in the driveway?' My dad has been working seven days a week since the war began. Actually, Alfred has only seen his car a couple of times.

Dad is a glutton for work, especially since the war began and he is working at the shipyard. He works lots of overtime so he's gone in the morning before I get up and doesn't come home at night till after bedtime. Mom and Dad have never had so much money. He said when school starts this year, he'll raise Duane's and my allowance from twenty-five cents twice a month to fifty cents a week. Duane and I almost couldn't believe our ears. Dad's pretty tight with money and Mom has to make sure the money lasts from payday to payday.

"Yeah, that's his car. Kinda crazy. He's never home during the day. Something must have happened!"

I'm getting a little nervous. Mom and I have been home from our "pear picking vacation" to Potter Valley for only a week. Thinking about the last week, it seems like there has been a lot of talking coming from Mom and Dad's bedroom. That's strange, too.

We can hear Mom and Dad talking as we walk up the back stairs and come into the kitchen. They stop talking as we enter. Dad has "that look". Like when he's about to get the belt and whip one of us. Mom has been crying. Her eyes are red and watery. I know we've got to get out of here.

"Mom, Alfred and I just stopped to drop my books. We're going downtown to see if any new comic books have come in." It's the first thing I could think of to get away.

Dad turns and I can feel his eyes look right through me. "Take a chair son. What we're talking about affects you, too." Turning to Alfred, "You'd better be going Alfred. We're discussing a family matter".

Alfred is out the back door like a flash. He hasn't seen Dad when he's really upset. Dad's eyes turn to a piercing, steel gray and you seem to shrink as he stares at you. I sit at the kitchen table next to Mom. I don't know what to expect. My mind is racing back over the past week to remember anything I've done that would upset Dad.

Dad gets up, takes his cup to the stove and pours some coffee. Back at the table he adds some cream and two spoons full of sugar. He leans back in his chair. His eyes soften as he speaks. "Son, your mother has something she wants to tell you."

I look quizzically at Mom. She has a hanky in her hand and brushes it across her eyes. I don't think I want to be here. I'm pretty sure I don't want to hear what Mom has to say.

Mom takes a deep breath. "Boomie, your father and I have decided to move to Potter Valley. We've bought a pear farm not far from where you and I picked pears for the Whites. We'll be near your uncle Don and uncle Reed and your cousins."

I almost fall out of my chair. Dad starts wheezing like a wounded animal.

Mom goes on with some details but I'm not listening. This can't be true. Pinole is where all my friends live. Potter Valley is so small the school looked about the size of our house. No sidewalks for skating and riding scooters with my friends! No friends! I didn't see any tennis courts. No Alfred and his comic books. Nothing to do!

Finally, I hear her say, "We'll be moving next Saturday. Your great uncle Dee will be here with his truck and we'll have everything packed so we can make the move in one day."

I've got a million questions, mostly about why we have to move to that desolate place. Most of a month there this summer was too much for me, already. I try but can't speak. I'm stunned, shocked. I don't even think about all the great times Duane and I had each summer when we visited Grandma and Grandpa on their farm and played with uncle Tex. That was different, anyway. It was just for the summer. And it was with uncle Tex. All my other uncles are "old men".

"Your father finished his work at the shipyard this morning and will be getting everything ready to move during the week. You and your brothers and sister will stay in school here till Friday. We'll get transfers so there's no problem entering school in Potter Valley."

I look at Mom. Her eyes are still wet. Something went on between Mom and Dad before I got here. I look back at Dad. He has kind of a smile on his face now. It's like a plot. They've been ganging up on us kids and now we all have to leave our friends and live in "the sticks".

Mom continues. "Your brother, Duane, is already in Potter and is staying with uncle Don till we get there." I thought Duane was starting high school in Richmond this week. I've been so busy with Alfred I don't even know what's happening around here.

I can think of only one thing. I don't want to leave Pinole. The baseball field is just across the street. So are the tennis courts. My friends for the past seven years all live within three or four blocks. We skate together; play kick-the-can. We build scooters. Mom and Dad don't know it but I've got a girlfriend named Beth. Her mother works at the bank. Because Uncle Fred worked there, Duane and I bowl free at the Hercules Powder Plant on the two alleys in the basement.

The more I think, the closer I come to crying.

Then I remember what Mom always says when things go wrong. I've heard it a thousand times. She says, "Boomie, get a piece of paper and pencil and sit down. Now, pencil a line down the center of the paper. Now write 'bad' on the left and 'good' on the right. Write down everything in your life that's bad in the left column. Then write down all the good things in the right column."

I've had to do that more times than I can remember. Every time there's only a couple or three things in the "bad" column and a whole bunch of stuff in the "good" column. I don't want to have to do that now.

I try to think of something good. The first good thing is that I won't have to go to Richmond every week for church. That's become a real drag.

It's a whole 'nuther story.

It was the first Sunday after school vacation started. Duane had already gone to Potter Valley. Dad was working like he did most Sundays since the war began. Without a car, Mom didn't want to take the bus to church with me and my little brother and sister. But she wanted me to attend. I'd been baptized and just after my twelfth birthday I was ordained a "Deacon", so I had responsibilities at the Sunday service. I argued. Mom won.

We'd had an early summer rain Saturday night. It stopped Sunday morning but everything was pretty wet. I dressed in my only "grownup kid suit" and took the bus to Richmond where we attended church. It was about three blocks from the bus stop to the church. The bus was a little late arriving and I didn't want to be late for the start of Sunday School that began an hour before the "adult service" so I decided to run.

It went okay until I had to cross a vacant block along a dirt path. Well, it was usually dirt. This morning it was a "mud" path. Yep! About half way across I slipped and skidded about six feet in a pool of water and mud. When I got up, I was a mess.

I tried to wipe as much mud off my suit as possible. I tried using water from the pools to wash clumps of mud off. Wet, streaks of mud, one really discouraged "Deacon"! I'd just about decided to go home. Then I heard Mom's words. "People won't make fun of you as long as they know you're doing your best." Well, I decided right there to do my best. Wet, mud-streaked suit, I went on to church.

Mom had never been so wrong. Before I even got up the front steps, I heard giggles and people were pointing at me. Inside you'd think I had leprosy. A high schooler asked me who washes my clothes.

Before the Sunday School service even began, I'd been so taunted and ridiculed that I knew I'd made a really big mistake. I bolted for the exit, leaving the congregation to find some other interest.

That Sunday I realized that I didn't want to be around these types of people. It took that incident, in a long line of other bad experiences, to result in my departure from that church as a teenager.

I'm still thinking about moving. I guess I'm looking pretty discouraged. Dad gets up and puts a hand on my shoulder. Mostly I don't like to talk to Dad. It's almost always bad news and the belt. This is different. His touch is soft and light. His eyes shine a little from wetness. I get the feeling this isn't exactly what Dad had in mind, either.

He speaks. "Son, we've worked hard as a family so that someday we can have a place of our own. While you and your mother were in Potter Valley, she found a nice farm with everything we'll need to make a good living. We've bought it and we're going to be farmers. I know you're thinking of all your friends here. It may not seem like it but soon you'll have friends just like them in Potter Valley. When I was your age, I had about the same experience. Seemed terribly wrong to me at the time but it worked out okay."

I knew that Dad's father had left him alone with his sister and his mom when he was in the sixth grade. He had to quit school and go to work to help support the family. I was already in seventh grade. I guess back then, things had been really tough for him.

I've never 'talked back' to Dad. This is different. I look up at him. "I'm not going. I'm going to stay here with Alfred and his dad." I'd stayed over at Alfred's place lots of times and it was home to me. I expect Dad to react with a smack across my face.

Instead, he sits down and pulls his chair right up to me. He never did anything like this before. "Son, we're a family and we'll stay together. If you like, we'll agree right now to invite Alfred to spend next summer with us on the farm. You'll be able to show him a whole new life. There'll be lots of hunting and fishing and hiking. In fact, a river runs right next to our farm and a creek runs right through it. Both have plenty of fish, winter and summer. There are deer, ducks, pheasant and quail to hunt. It'll be different than life here, of course, but I think you'll find it is lots of fun."

As soon as Dad mentioned Alfred and hunting my mind started going a million miles an hour. Alfred and I will have our pistol. We can be gangsters, or cowboys, or crooks, or anything we want. With so few people we will be able to shoot our pistol almost anywhere. We might even get a wild rabbit or something.

Suddenly I feel Mom and Dad both staring at me. It's quiet. I look at Mom. She has that kinda 'hopeful' look on her face like she does when she's going to give me a hug or something. Dad's waiting for me to say something.

A minute ago I was too shocked to cry. I feel kind of mad, like I've been betrayed. Still, I know there's really nothing I can do. And the thought of having the pistol and the summer with Alfred keeps flashing into my mind.

Then I think of today in school with Mrs. Jordan. No matter what, seventh grade in Potter Valley can't be any worse than having Mrs. Jordan. Suddenly I feel free. I won't do any of the homework she assigned. I'll just be on vacation, in school, for a week while my friends suffer with all the homework and quizzes.

"I know I won't like it. What do you want me to do?" Actually, through my anger and surprise I'm starting to get a little excited. I think of Mom's list of "bad and good" things. I figure there will be at least some good things about the wretched little valley we're moving to.

And now I know why Mom insisted Duane give up the paper route before school started.

I want to go out and start telling my friends that I'll be leaving. I don't want to hear any more from Mom and Dad right now. I need to think and talk to Alfred. I get up to leave.

Mom says, "Boomie, make sure you're here at 5:00 o'clock for dinner. Your little brother and sister haven't been told we're moving yet and we'd like you to be here when we tell them."

"Okay Mom. I'll be here in plenty of time." I think, what am I supposed to do, cheer or something? I'm out of there. I can hear Mom and Dad talking about the move as I go down the front stairs and hop onto my bike. I'm hoping that Alfred will be home as I pedal as fast as I can along Valley Road to his house.

Alfred's dad is working on his motorcycle as I ride up. "How was your first day of school with Mrs. Jordan?" Everyone knows about Mrs. Jordan's reputation.

"Okay! Is Alfred home?" I don't have time for 'small talk' right now, even though I love to talk to Alfred's dad. I know what I want and I've never been so determined.

"He's upstairs in his library of comic books. Just go right in." Alfred's dad always treats me like a member of the family. I couldn't even think of doing what I'm about to do if he weren't a 'Cool Dad'.

Alfred's on his bed, surrounded by comic books. I say, "Hi". He jumps. I guess I was pretty quiet coming up the stairs.

"Hi Boomie. Thought you'd be studying all the stuff the old lady gave us. What's up?"

I sit down next to Alfred and explain what has happened; that I'm moving away. He doesn't say a word. Then I explain the good part. "My dad said that you can come and spend all next summer with us on our farm. He says we'll be able to fish in the river that runs right through our place and even do some hunting."

Alfred is "with it" immediately. "Hey, maybe I can come up for Christmas vacation. We could explore and plan everything for summer." That's what I like about Alfred. He always makes the best of everything.

Before I can even respond he's off the bed and down the stairs to tell his dad. I'm right behind him. Sure enough, his dad is as excited as he is before even asking where our farm is.

I decide it's time. "The other reason I came out here is to see if I can take our pistol with me when I move. Dad said that everybody hunts in the valley and I know my brother, Duane got a couple of deer just before school started." I'm a little nervous. What if Alfred's dad decides to talk to my father? Wow!

I wait. I can see that Alfred's dad is thinking. Finally, he puts down the wrench he was using and says, "You know, that's a good idea. Out in the country is the right place for you boys to learn to properly use that pistol. Just remember what the sheriff told you, both!"

I almost faint with relief. It's working. I'm going to have the pistol. We go into the house. Alfred's dad opens a trunk in the corner of the kitchen and hands me the bag, pistol inside. My hand is shaking as I take it and put it into my backpack. Alfred is talking a mile a minute about everything we're going to do with the pistol when he visits me on the farm. I just want to get out of here before something changes. I don't even know how I'm going to get the pistol hidden in my stuff for the move. But I know I am. Even the thought of Dad's belt doesn't bother me.

Finally, Alfred's dad goes out to continue working on his motorcycle. Alfred and I are alone. "You know, Boomie, I've got some bullets for the pistol."

I can't believe what I'm hearing. We'd used all the bullets the first day with Alfred's dad and the sheriff.

"Where'd you get them?"

"You know Joey who works in the butcher shop at Ruff's? Well, he comes out every week or so to Silva's ranch where he butchers pigs and steers for the meat market. I was there getting milk one day when he came out. I wanted to see what he did so he let me go with him into the pen.

He's got a 38 pistol, just like ours. Uses it to shoot the pig or steer right in the middle of its forehead before he cuts its throat. Well, while he was busy skinning a steer I walked by his pickup. He had a big box full of bullets in his pickup so I just took a few. He had so many I knew he wouldn't miss them.

I've got them hidden right here in my room. I decided it was better if Dad didn't know, this time."

Alfred digs a paper bag out from under a stack of comics and hands it to me. Sure enough, about 15 bullets. I don't know if I'm happy or scared. Maybe both!

How can I know now that what's been a "disastrous day" will lead to the greatest adventures of my life?

CHAPTER 15 – "COUNTRY BUMPKIN"

You change pretty fast when you ain't got no choice. It's Saturday morning. The pistol and bullets are hidden in my backpack. They've been there all week, along with a baseball, my baseball glove and some tennis balls. I stuffed a couple of baseball caps in, too, just for good measure. I keep the backpack with me as we all load into the car.

Our old Plymouth follows Uncle Dee's truck all the way from Pinole to Potter Valley. It's about four hours. Uncle Dee's truck just has sideboards so all our stuff is covered with a canvas that he and Dad tied down to the truck bed. A couple of times the canvas gets loose, flapping in the wind, and little things fall off the truck. Dad honks and honks till Uncle Dee stops so we can go back and pick up our stuff and tie the load down again. The last hour we travel through a wilderness canyon alongside a river. No homes, no people, no nothing.

The whole trip is kinda like dinner. No one talks. Duane's already in the valley, so he's not with us. My little brother and sister sit in the corners of the back seat reading and looking out the car window. I like to sleep when I'm riding in the car. Not this time. I'm watching Uncle Dee's truck and looking for where we're going to finally stop.

We drive through the "town" of Potter Valley. I see two saloons, one store, a post office, a tiny grammar school and a smaller high school. We are through town before I know it. I thought Pinole was small.

About a mile north of town Uncle Dee pulls into a dirt driveway that goes about a quarter mile back to our 'new home'.

We all get out of the car. I guess Dad wants to be funny. "Welcome to the Foster Castle".

I can't believe what I see. "Is this our house?"

Mom answers, "It's only temporary, Boomie. We'll fix it up."

I gotta tell you about this place. All I've known is 'city life', at least since I was in kindergarten. In the houses we rented we push a switch and the lights come on. Or we turn a handle and the heat comes on. We have faucets to get hot and cold water when we do dishes or take a bath. Nature calls and we use the bathroom.

I think, it can't be as bad on the inside as the outside. No paint. Holes in the walls! Holes in the roof! And it stinks! The barn and house are almost right together.

My little brother and sister just stand, starring.

I run into the house to look for the bathroom. It only takes a minute. There are four tiny rooms, no sinks, no lights, no faucets, an old wood stove in one room – the kitchen, I guess – and no bathroom. None at all! I turn to leave. A squirrel runs out the door ahead of me.

Uncle Dee sees what I'm looking for. "Boy" he says. He always calls me "Boy". "Just go out behind the barn and hang it out".

That stops me. "Mom, where's the bathroom?"

Mom looks at Dad. "We're in the country now, Son. It's a little different, but you'll get used to it. For now, do what Uncle Dee says."

I'm thinking, this can't be. When we stayed with Uncle Don just a month ago, he had a bathroom with water, electric lights, a gas stove to cook – everything I'm used to."

My little sister has been listening. She starts crying. Now Mom has the problem. My sister asks, "What do I do?"

I'm not sure exactly how it works, but Mom got a roll of toilet paper and she took my sister out behind the barn. My sister was giggling when she returned, so I guess it was okay. I decided to "hold it" for a while.

Uncle Dee is untying the load. Dad and I venture onto the back porch. There's a 'hand pump' with a bucket of water sitting alongside. He dumps some water down an opening and begins pumping furiously. Pretty soon water gushes out of the pump, into the bucket.

"That's how we get water, Son." He got another bucket. "Here, you try. It's all primed so you won't need to pour water down it."

I'm still in denial. That's our water supply, outside, from under the ground. Pour some water down the top and pump the handle as fast as you can. Pretty soon water comes out the spout.

I pump a bucket full but don't stop fast enough and water splashes everywhere.

It's Mom. "It's okay, Boomie. You'll learn how."

She's told me stories of how it was when she was young on the farm with all her brothers and sisters. At least, they had a 'outhouse'. We don't even have one of them. "Boomie, we're all going to have to adjust a little. Your dad is going to build an 'out-house' first thing. For now, we'll just 'do what we need to' out behind the barn, like Uncle Dee says. It'll take a while but we'll be getting lights and water in the house."

Dad grips my hand and says, "Come with me, son." We leave the back porch and walk out into the pear orchard that is located just beyond several apple trees that border the house. The "front" orchard: 4 acres. The harvest was just completed and there are a few "stragglers" left on the trees that were too small during the picking season.

Dad pauses as we enter the first tree line. "Look around son".

I look down the rows of trees. Then see the edges of the creek that flows through the orchard. I turn, and see the bridge, under which I can hear the water from the river that borders our property. Along the road is a fence, covered with blackberry bushes.

Dad speaks. "Son, out there along the creek and river banks you'll see wild rabbits and wild ducks." We move toward the fence and patches of blackberries. A swarm of quail fly out of the berries. "Quail make their nests in the blackberries. You'll see them by the ton, year-around."

We walk down to the bridge. "The river is full of trout and perch. And, when it rains in the winter, the salmon swim up the river to spawn; all winter and spring."

I stand and stare at the water flowing over the small dam.

Dad continues. "Alfred's dad stopped by to see me yesterday. He told me about the pistol you and Alfred found."

I'm shocked; about to run back to the house. Dad puts his hand on my shoulder. "Don't worry. Things have changed. We're in the country now. He told me how he and the sheriff spent time with you two, showing you how to care for and be proper owners of a gun. Out here, you'll be using that pistol to bring home wild rabbits for food."

I remember the many times I was whipped because I didn't remember to cut grass for the rabbits we used to raise in Pinole.

Then Dad really shocked me. "You remember my shotgun? Well, I'm giving it to you so you'll be able to bring home some of the ducks and quail we've seen. It won't take long for you to become a "sharp shooter". We'll practice together as soon as we're settled in to our new home."

I look at my father in disbelief. My world has changed in an instant. No whipping for the pistol. My own shotgun. I'm now starring into my dad's eyes. He continues: "Duane has been here all summer working for your uncles Don and Reed. He has his own rifle, a 25/35 that he uses for deer hunting. He's already gotten a couple that have supplied plenty of meat for your uncles and families. We'll get you a similar rifle, soon, so you can hunt deer with your brother."

We start back to our "house" to help with the unloading. I'm stunned. Maybe it won't be so bad, after all. I'm still shocked that

Dad actually talked with me like this. I feel like I'm dreaming and I'm afraid I'll awaken.

As we arrive back at the house. Uncle Dee, Mom and my siblings are busily taking stuff from the car and truck into our "new house". Dad gets the shotgun from the cab of Uncle Dee's truck and hands it to me. "Keep this in your bedroom with your pistol. It's yours now."

An hour later, Uncle Dee is gone. "Stuff" is all over the back porch and scattered in the yard and house. No matter what just happened, it's going to take a while to adjust. I didn't know it then, but with that conversation with Dad, all of the belt and strap whippings were behind me. Never again, for either Duane or me.

Little did I know at that moment that we'd have to harvest next year's pear crop before we'd have any of those 'city conveniences' in the house again. With my pistol and my new shotgun, I don't really care.

So, here's how we "settle in" to make it work!

Mom, Dad and my little sister share one 'bedroom'. Duane, my little brother and I share the other. They're small rooms – wall-towall beds. No closets! No room for our dressers! Dressers on the back porch! String a rope on the back porch to hang our clothes. Mom has a 'washboard' to do the laundry with a big round tub to rinse clothes.

The big round tub pulls double duty as our bathtub on Saturday nights. Bath water comes from the pump on the back porch. Hot water comes from a pot on the wood stove in the kitchen. First guy to bathe gets the clean water.

Dad builds a chicken coop with an 'outhouse' behind it. A two holer! Never have figured out why there were two holes. At night, our light comes from an oil lantern in the middle of the kitchen table.

My first thought is, "I can't have Alfred up for Christmas or spend the summer with me here. He'll think my whole family has gone crazy."

Well, that thought didn't last long. No choice! I adapt.

I'm not sure about going to a new school. I've been in the Pinole school since kindergarten. Knew all the teachers and all my friends. Now I don't know anybody.

I checked out the school over the weekend. It's really small. But, it's the biggest building in town. What a hick place.

Monday morning I'm getting ready for school. We've had breakfast. Mom says she'll take us. Not me!

"Mom, I'm going to leave for school now." It's only 8 o'clock and school starts at 9. "I know where everything is, so it's okay." I've got my transfer from Pinole.

Mom replies, "Boomie, I'm taking your brother and sister to school so if you need anything I'll be there". She knows I don't want "my mom" taking me to the first day of school. Not in the seventh grade.

It's a mile to town, so I take off walking. Duane, who has been in the valley working all summer, has already been going to high school for a week. He's the fifteenth student in a four-year high school. That's less than four kids per grade. At least they have three rooms for different classes.

Mom's already there with my little brother and sister when I arrive. The school looks kinda like a bigger version of our house. I go in the front door and almost run into a little guy.

"You must be Boomie Foster! I'm Don Dashiel. Your uncle told me you were coming."

I'm not sure how to react. I say, "Yep!"

"Come with me. I'll show you where our room is." He turns the corner. I follow. About ten steps and we're in the classroom.

A teacher is there. Don says, "Mr. Walton, this is our new student". Mr. Walton is the principal. I quickly find out he's also my teacher.

I've never had a man for a teacher. Not only that, he tells me I'm in class with sixth and eighth graders. Don disappears.

The grammar school has only three rooms for eight grades. My little sister is in the first grade with the second grade. My little brother is in the third grade with the fourth and fifth grades.

When we left Pinole the "School on the Hill" had two rooms for every grade and about fifty students in each room. Almost a thousand students! After the war started, it really grew.

Now there aren't fifty students in the whole grammar school. What a "hick" place!

I give Mr. Walton the paper that has all my school stuff on it. He asks, "Do you want to be called Rodney or Rod"?

"Everybody calls me Boomie, so that's okay". He just nods.

It doesn't take long to find out a thing or two. In the classroom I've got to stand up and introduce myself and tell everybody about my family, where we're from and why we've moved to "this stinking little valley".

I guess I don't make much of an impression, at least on one of my seventh-grade classmates. After a couple of hours, the bell announces the lunch hour. Kids scatter. I eat my bagged lunch, a sandwich and an apple at my desk. I decide to see the playground. In Pinole each grade had their own area, usually a small baseball field.

Welcome to the country!

I'm barely out in the playground and I meet Bean Miller. Later I learn he's an American Indian and lives on a reservation in the valley. I've never seen a real Indian before. He grabs me from behind and throws me to the ground. "How's that feel, 'city dude'?

I struggle. He sits on me, laughing. He's not "that" much bigger than me but right now he looks like a giant. "Lemme up!"

He likes to fight (whoever he can beat), and I'm his newest target. I've never been in a schoolyard fight in my life. In Pinole, we all grew up together, all friends and no one ever fought.

Finally, two of my new classmates pull him off my struggling body and help me up. I'm ready to go home. Enough of this, already! I'm really embarrassed.

Lunch recess ends. We go back into class.

My hope fades when there's not a word about the fight. My problem and my plight! I guess this kind of stuff happens all the time. No one cares. Bean Miller sits behind me and laughs. I ignore him but I begin to think of what I'm going to have to do to keep from getting beat up.

I've got my pistol at home. Maybe I can scare him. Then I think what the sheriff said. Never point a gun unless you intend to use it. I know I'm not going to shoot anybody, not even Bean.

I've got to do something. I'm not going to come to school to get beat up by Bean Miller every day.

An idea begins to jell.

My big brother, Duane, was always my role model. Even though he's three years older I always tried to follow him and his friends around and hang out with them. During Easter break this year he, Jim Bradley and Buster Nelson got interested in boxing after they saw a movie about a boxer named "Gentleman Jim Corbett". Instead of just standing there beating on each other, Jim Corbett ducked, dodged and danced so his opponent couldn't hit him square. Then he'd swoop in and land a couple of really good ones. He kept winning his fights and didn't get hit much or hurt.

Buster had some boxing gloves so the three of them practiced boxing in the vacant lot next to Jim Bradley's house. I watched them all week. I'd ask them to let me box but they kept saying I was too little.

The more I watched the more I wanted to be a boxer. By Friday they were getting pretty good at dodging punches, then bouncing in and smashing each other With the padded boxing gloves, no one got hurt.

Finally, when they'd finished that Friday, and after I kept pleading with them to let me try, Jim said he'd box with me. I was really excited. Wanting to be careful and make sure I didn't get really hurt, Duane took Jim's gloves and said I could box with him.

I put on the gloves and Buster tied the strings. I was ready. I jumped around, danced back and forth and we began the match. Man, it was quick. In no time at all Duane had banged me in the stomach, smacked me in the chest and almost knocked my head off with his short, quick jabs.

I guess he got so involved he didn't realize how hard he was punching. The next thing I knew I was on my back, on the ground and all three of them were trying to get me up. Knocked groggy. Blood was trickling out of my nose and into my mouth.

Duane was really upset with himself. He kept saying how sorry he was and how he didn't mean to knock me down. After a minute I felt okay and my nose stopped bleeding. Buster took the gloves off of me. I got up.

He didn't have to, but Duane got me to promise I wouldn't mention this to Mom or Dad. If I did, I knew we'd both get it much worse than a little bloody nose.

Over that weekend, Duane borrowed the boxing gloves and we practiced for hours. We even had a jump rope we used to practice our foot movements. By Monday when we went back to school, I was feeling pretty good about my boxing.

Duane and I got so busy with school, chores and baseball that I didn't box any more. And then summer came and Duane went to Potter Valley.

Duane is a sophomore at the high school. I think, if I can get him to teach me more about boxing, maybe it will solve the problem with Bean Miller. I've got to do something, quick. Something I can do right now. At recesses I'll have to hang out with other guys from my class. That may make Bean think before attacking me.

After school I meet Duane back at our farm. We're supposed to shovel out the irrigation ditches around the front orchard. I sit on the bank, head between my knees. Duane is shoveling. I never shirk my part of our chores so Duane knows something's wrong.

"Okay Boomie, what happened?"

I'm not sure how to begin. Duane's a pretty protective big brother. I start, "I had kind of a problem at school with Bean Miller. He's the Indian."

Duane already knows Bean, and his grandfather, Bob. He hardly ever says anything bad about anyone, so I'm surprised at what he says. "Yeh, I met Bean just after I got here. Uncle Reed had some hay to put up and hired Bean to do it. I was working for Uncle Don. The first day Bean moved one wagon load from the field into the barn and Uncle Reed fired him. What a flake! What did he do to you?"

"I was kinda surprised. At lunch recess he comes up, slugs me, grabs me and throws me down. I don't even know him. Then he holds me down till a couple of classmates pull him off." I'm almost ashamed to admit this, even to Duane.

Duane puts his shovel down. "Okay, let's go to the reservation, now. We'll make sure Bean knows who he's fooling with. He'll find out that we stick together. If any of the others want to get involved, I know uncle Reed and uncle Don will back us up."

There's no way I want a confrontation now. And we both know Duane can't always be around to protect me. This is all new and I'm not sure exactly what to say. I'm really happy that Duane wants to even the score yet, somehow, I know I've got to do this myself.

"Duane, you're a great brother and I'm really glad that you're ready to help me. But, somehow I've got to do this myself. Bean and I are going to be in school together all year. You can't be around all the time to be my bodyguard." He already knows that.

I go on to let Duane know that I didn't really get hurt; it was just embarrassing. After a while, Duane agrees that beating up on Bean won't help since I've got to face him at school, anyway.

I remain sitting. Duane is leaning on his shovel, thinking. Suddenly he shouts, "I've got it."

I look up. "Got what?"

Duane explains. It seems that when he arrived in Potter Valley early in the summer he met a boy his age, Jim Corbell. They became immediate friends and horseback riding pals. Jim was from the city, too. He's small and he'd started practicing Jujitsu so he could defend himself against the bigger "farm boys". He was really happy to have Duane so they could practice with each other. Jim had a book that showed all the holds and moves. In their spare time, they worked out together and by the end of summer they both were pretty good.

"With Jujitsu, size doesn't matter. In fact, the smaller guy has an advantage in most of the jujitsu moves."

I'm really listening now. After our boxing experience, I'm ready to consider anything. Duane says, "I know I can teach you two or three of the basic moves. It'll only take a few hours and I'm sure you will be able to use them, okay. Let's start your training right now."

Duane moves over to the grassy area between the pear trees and calls me to follow. Suddenly he grabs my left forearm, does a little spin, leans over and 'whap', I'm on the ground on my back, looking up at him.

"What was that?" I'm shocked. It happened so fast.

Duane explains. "That's just one of the jujitsu moves Jim and I practiced this summer. See how easy it was to throw you down. There are about four other grips and moves that work just as well, from the front, side or back. It's all about leverage."

We have maybe three hours before dark. This is going to have to be fast.

Duane works with me for a couple of hours.

Mom calls us to dinner. Duane agrees to work out with me tomorrow. I'm feeling really great. Maybe there is something I can do about Bean Miller.

I remember when Duane first learned to play tennis. He had just turned eight. I was five. Uncle Fred, who was a good tennis player, taught him and his friends. I watched them every chance I got. It looked so easy. A big racket and a soft ball! Lots easier than baseball, with the little bat and the hard ball. I knew I could do it. We played baseball all the time.

One day when Duane's friends, Jim Bradley and Buster Nelson were playing, I asked if I could play, too. Jim gave me his tennis racket and said, "have at it, Boomie." They both knew I'd never played tennis before. It only took a few minutes to find out that it was a lot harder than I thought to hit that fast-moving tennis ball, even with the big racket. Buster kept hitting the balls to me and I'd swing and miss, swing and miss. Then, when I finally connected, I hit the ball out into the street.

They laughed and laughed. Jim took his racket from me and I left, head hanging. How could hitting that ball be so hard when it looked so easy?

Later that day I told Duane what had happened. Just like he always did, he took me out to the court and I got my first lesson in tennis. He showed me how to grip the racket, how to keep the wrist stiff, how to keep the elbow close in, how to swing backhand and how to reach and serve.

I had the fundamentals. My uncle Fred agreed to play tennis with me if I would play Monopoly with him. I agreed, and we did. So, I got lessons from uncle Fred, too. Now, all I needed was a partner to practice. Yep, Alfred was excited about learning tennis, too. For the next month Alfred and I were on the courts whenever no one else was there, practicing all the moves. When the courts were in use, we used a wall next to the firehouse to practice against.

I quickly learned to love tennis, and got pretty good at all the strokes. Alfred and I didn't tell anyone else. Tennis was "our secret".

Then one afternoon we walked over to the tennis courts when Jim Bradley and Buster Nelson were playing. Duane was sitting on the bench, waiting to play the winner. Because of Uncle Fred's training, Duane was a ton better than either Jim or Buster; he always won.

As we sat next to Duane, Buster asked why we were there. No hesitation, Alfred said "We're here to beat you and Jim at a game of doubles!" No backing down for Alfred, never.

Jim jumped over the net and said, "Let's go, boys. Show us how to play".

They had no idea we actually knew how to play, and in fact, played the game about as well as they did. Within just minutes they realized they'd have to play their best to beat us. We couldn't smash the ball as hard as they, but we were fast on the court and could return most anything they sent our way. Lots of long rallies! They'd win a point; we'd win a point.

When we'd played six games, they'd won three; Alfred and I'd won three.

We stopped and thanked them for the match. We weren't sure, but we thought that the longer we played the better our chances of beating them. We didn't want that. It was enough that we'd played to a draw; they're Duane's friends and we like to "hang out" with all of them. Anyway, Alfred and I both had chores to do.

But I'd learned that with a good teacher and a commitment to practice, it was easy to learn something new.

I figured it would take about a week of practice with Duane before I'd be able to deal with Bean.

Can a person learn in their sleep? All night I'm dreaming about how I'm going to take Bean down when he attacks me. From the front; from the side; from behind! Every move is quick, smooth and final.

By morning, when I'm doing the chores, I know I can do it. On the way to school Duane and I talk. He's telling me to just keep my distance from Bean for a day or two. We'll practice after school and it won't be long till I'll be ready.

It's tough being a new kid in a new school, even a small school with just a few other students. Between classes and at recesses I hang out with Don Dashiell, who was the first to befriend me, and Lee Walton, our teacher's son. That seems to keep Bean "at bay". No problem.

After our practice Tuesday afternoon Duane says, "Boomie, you're ready, already. Let Bean come after you. Do what you've been doing to me and you'll be able to throw him down and have him in a hold most every time he tries to get you."

Wednesday morning, I walk to school with Duane. I am confident. I feel six feet tall and two hundred pounds. For the first time in this school, I feel good. I'm ready for Bean Miller.

PART TWO EPILOGUE:

THE BULLY

Introduction to Potter Valley Grade School

<u>City Dude to Country Warrior</u>

When I was just a little boy, as skinny as can be,
most people looked as large as sin and much too strong for me.
It didn't help when every time I messed up just a bit,
a belt was used across my butt until I couldn't sit.

I lived in a small town with lots of children all around.
We climbed the hills, played kick the can and wrestled on the ground.
Most everyone was playful, just young kids, all having fun.
Sometimes we rang a doorbell then we'd turn and really run.

I lived this way till I was twelve and then I went away.
My family bought a little farm, with pears and cows and hay.
I went to school, the seventh grade, the place was new to me.
I'm growing tall, but still quite small, and thin as I can be.

With only three rooms in the school, the place was pretty small.
That's not a lot of kids to meet, one day, I knew them all.
I quickly knew that I had learned a lot more than my peers.
The school down in the city was ahead by months, or years.

The lessons were a snap for me; I knew them very well.
The other kids soon understood that I was no dumbbell.
So, I felt really good, for in the classroom I would shine.
New friends, new school, no problems, I was really doing fine.

Then just like that, first day at noon, right in the yard at school.
A guy I'd met but didn't know, taught me "the country rule".
Bean Miller was his name and he looked big and very tall.
I got one in the gut, then on the chin, that made me fall.

99

I'd never had to fight before; this thing was new to me.
And standing there above me, he seemed larger than a tree.
Up on my knees I tried to stand; he threw me to the ground.
I guess he didn't like it that I hadn't made a sound.

The lunch hour finally ended; I was saved; we went inside.
I focused on just one thing now, how I could save my hide.
I knew I didn't do a thing provoking that attack.
Yet there I was, holding my gut and lying on my back.

When school was out, I got my books and ran home to our farm.
I'd tried to stay away from him so he'd not do me harm.
Yet, he was sure that I'd return; I had to be at school.
I had no clue what I could do; it wasn't very cool.

My brother, Duane, met me at home;
knew there was something wrong.
He usually found me outgoing, humming a folk song.
Today I hunched down on the bank, my face between my knees.
He thought I'd be out in the orchard, working in the breeze.

"What's wrong there, Boomie?
You look like you've lost your only friend."
"First day at school was kind of tough; thought it would never end."
We talked about Bean Miller and the incident at school.
I didn't know what I should do; I felt just like a fool.

Duane jumped up, grabbed my arm, saying that he could help me,
quick!
I followed him just like a sheep, though I was feeling sick.
He and a friend, during the summer, practiced jujitsu.
He said, "I learned it pretty good; I know I can teach you".

Three hours later, in the orchard, I was "throwing Duane".
He showed me how to make the moves, avoiding any pain.
And better, it works best when one is smaller than his foe.
I wouldn't have to wait for years to let my body grow.

He said we'd practice the next day, until I knew each hold.
He'd let me "throw him down" until I had the system cold.
Just stay with students who are friends tomorrow at grade school.
You'll be ready by Wednesday to make Bean Miller the fool.

So, Tuesday I stayed close to two classmates that I had met.
Bean Miller stayed his distance; made it through without a sweat.
At home I practiced jujitsu with Duane into the night.
More confidence with every "throw"; I'm ready for the fight.

I greeted school on Wednesday with great happiness and glee.
I know that from this "bully" I'll no longer have to flee.
I met Bean Miller at the gate before classes began.
We stood there eye to eye, for I felt every bit a man.

He made one move; I grabbed his arm, my head against his chin.
I threw him down; he knew at once; this fight he couldn't win.
He tried again, I grabbed his arm, one roll, he's on the ground.
He's moaning as he holds his leg, and that's his only sound.

I have his arm behind his back till there is no more bend.
The words come quickly from Bean's mouth,
"I want to be your friend".
He laughs a little; struggles free and reaches for my hand.
I took it into mine; we shook. Now that felt really grand.

I guess I learned a bully doesn't bully any more,
as soon as he finds out that you can even up the score.
I went to school, yes, every day, at recess we all played.
Old Bean and I are now good friends and friends we've always
stayed.

GUNS AND RIFLES
CHRISTMAS WITH ALFRED

I didn't know at the time that Dad talked to me in the front orchard that he had already "greased the skids" so to speak, getting Alfred's Dad's okay for him to spend Christmas vacation with us, in just three months. Although Alfred and I had talked about his visiting us on the farm, I didn't believe it would ever happen. My whole world changed after that "very first ever" real discussion with Dad.

It happened right on schedule. Alfred arrived the Saturday following the beginning of two weeks of Christmas vacation. The timing was perfect. In the winter, the orchard requires only tree pruning. Dad gave me "time off".

The first couple of days, Alfred and I explored the creek and river on our property. We carried the pistol and shotgun so Alfred could become acquainted with how they are actually used in a "hunting" environment. As usual, Alfred adapted quickly. Just like in sports he played, he soon learned to rest the shotgun across his elbow, take aim and squeeze the trigger.

Then, for the remainder of the two weeks Alfred and I lived with the pistol, the shotgun and my 32/20 rifle. I'd already become pretty proficient with all three, though the shotgun "kicked" pretty hard when it was fired. A Winchester pump with a 32 inch, full choke barrel. But, with it, you could bring down a rapidly departing quail from over 75 yards away.

Every evening we returned from our hunting expeditions along the creek and river to give Mom some "game" we'd shot or caught during our adventures. Fish, ducks, rabbits or quail. We even hunted for deer in the foothills about a mile from our farm, but since it was winter, the deer remained higher up in the mountains.

Nonetheless, both Alfred and I had the times of our lives. Christmas vacation ended way too soon.

Alfred returned to Pinole with stories he would tell to his classmates and friends for months to come. I returned to what had become an exciting life on the farm, doing things I'd never dreamed of before. Yes, there were lots of chores to be done, and school. But now, I had several close friends with whom I regularly hunted, fished and did other "stuff" that can be done only in the country.

Yes, Alfred had been my best friend through grade school. Now, each older, and each with other "best friends", it was quite natural that our lives moved on down separate trails. That Christmas vacation together was not only a long lasting, and wonderful memory, but it turned out to be the last time I ever saw Alfred. The paths of our lives simply took different directions.

Unknown to me at the time, those two weeks with Alfred represented the catalyst that began a long love affair with rifles and guns.

With years of experience hunting with rifles and shotguns, less than a decade later, as an accomplished expert Army Rifleman assigned to the 29th Infantry Regiment during the Korean War, I was the anchorman on the championship regimental rifle team that won the rifle competition among all of the military services in that Command.

That rifle competition served as a springboard for many additional life changing experiences as a member of the armed forces and beyond. That's another story!

PART THREE

LITTLE SKELETONS FROM A TEENAGER'S CLOSET
(Not Bad Kids – Maybe a Little Bad Behavior)

FRIENDS ARE BRAVE TOGETHER

When I was young, I didn't have a lot, yes, I was broke.
My dad worked for a buck a day, like lots of other folk.
The Great Depression; work was scarce, and not a lot of food.
An "attitude" is easy, as part of a hopeless brood.
I dreamed of many things I didn't have, but others did.
I even "tested limits", things my parents might forbid.
No "biggies", just the little stuff that lots of kids might do.
Yet I knew if I got caught, that I'd be in a "stew".

LET'S SMOKE
(4th grade)

My friend, Robert, stole a cigar; his father smoked the things.
We flew down to the creek, just like a bird with open wings.
Some matches in our pocket, we sat under a big tree.
We both wanted to smoke it first; we two could not agree.

So, Robert said he'd simply break that old cigar in two.
We'd each have half of that cigar; that's all we had to do.
We didn't have a knife so Robert broke it right in half.
He handed me a piece; it smelled so bad I had to laugh.

The broken ends were frayed; some of the leaves fell on the
ground.
But Robert "shushed" me quickly; didn't want a single sound.
If someone found us at the creek, smoking his dad's cigar,
I'd feel the belt across my legs till they would have a scar.

And Robert's dad would punish him by keeping him inside,
alone without a friend, until he'd wish that he had died.
We lit a match and each put our cigar into our mouth.
Then turned to face the north; the wind was blowing from the
south.

First, Robert puffed and puffed, and finally got his cigar lit.
I tried, I sucked and puffed until I lost my breath; I quit.
He lit another match; again, I tried to light that thing.
And just like that, smoke everywhere; so happy I could sing.

We puffed and laughed; a cloud of smoke surrounded both of us.
I coughed; the smoke now burned my eyes; filled my esophagus.
And Robert started choking; then he threw up on the ground.

With all of this commotion, I was sure that we'd be found.

We stomped on that cigar until there wasn't a bit left.
Both gagging, coughing, crying; we were totally bereft.
Back home I went into my room, I sat there on the bed.
I slumped; I felt all dizzy; put my arms across my head.

My mother came into the room; she knew something was wrong.
I moaned. I didn't know the cigar odor was so strong.
"Boy, you've been smoking, I can smell that stale, cigar smoke."
I tried to speak, I couldn't; every word made my throat choke.

She turned and left the room, and not another word was said.
Thank God, if she'd told Dad, I know that I'd rather be dead.
That day, Robert and I both learned a lesson; learned it quick.
Verboten were cigars and cigarettes; they make us sick.

And even though his mom and dad did not know what we'd tried.
We didn't tell them anything; it's not as though we'd lied.
And, even all our siblings didn't know what we had done.
"Our secret stayed a secret" learned a lesson; not much "fun"!

FIRST CAR – MY MODEL "A"

(High School Sophomore)

My sophomore year in high school; I was sixteen years of age.
And, owning one's own vehicle had now become the rage.
But money was a problem, for my parents had just split.
I had to go to school full time, I didn't want to quit.
With no allowance, just small jobs, I didn't have much hope.
I had a horse and bike; it looked like I'd just have to cope.
A neighbor gave me work so I could earn some extra cash.
I guarded every dollar; every week I'd count my stash.
Then when I had a hundred bucks, Dad took me for a drive.
A Model "A" for sale and it was only eighty-five.
I bought it on the spot and drove it home that very day,
about a hundred miles, although it seemed a long, long way.

One lucky guy, I bought a car and I was just sixteen.
A "Model A", two decades old, but it was "kinda" clean.
The engine leaked some oil, and the doors would barely shut.
The springs protruded through the seat, and scratched me on the
butt.
A radiator filled with oil; that should have let me know,
to get my "A" to run okay could take all of my dough.
But nothing mattered for I knew that I could make it run.
And, cruising with my friends was going to be a lot of fun.

So, every day in auto shop, I'd fix things that were wrong.
At night with friends, I'd drive around; we'd sing our high school
song.
Its body was gunmetal gray; the running boards were wood.
Before I left for town each night, I'd open up the hood.
The fenders rattled like a snake, all coiled and set to strike.
With nicks and dents most everywhere, they weren't at all alike.

The dollars that I earned were used to fix the things that broke;
gas leaking from the fuel pump or emitting too much smoke.
I somehow kept it running, as I replaced every part.
Dead battery or broken crank, I'd get my car to start.
My Model "A" could climb the hills and traverse all terrain.
But, when I tried to go too fast, the engine would complain.
For forty-five was maximum, and not a mile more,
and, even then the noise was something no one could ignore.
It took all of my money just to keep it running right.
My "A" took me to school by day; out with my friends by night.

We lived in a small valley, with about five hundred folk.
A few were "rich as Midas" but the rest were close to broke.
Most everyone helped everyone.
The work was spread around.
"Dirt farmers" mostly, milk their cows; they cultivate the ground.
Some farms had grapes and pears; a few had corn and some had
grain.
Most bought some water from "the district", supplementing rain.
Some farms were best known for the watermelons that they grew.
Huge fields with vines that produced watermelons by the slew!

The fields were fenced to keep the hungry coastal deer at bay.
They'd sometimes jump the fence and eat the melon vines like
hay.
Most farmers kept a shotgun on their front porch, just in case.
If deer came near their melon crop, the shotgun won the race.
It didn't kill the deer. It simply made them sting a bit.
A single shot was usually enough to make them quit.

There wasn't any place I wouldn't take my Model "A";
to school, to fish or hunt, even to haul some bailed hay.
It took my friends and me to all the games in which we played.
If distances were far away, then overnight we stayed.

There wasn't any one in town that didn't know my car.
No other car was like it; not a one was similar.
Some other kids had Model "A's", but none compared to mine,
for theirs had paint and windows, and the engines ran just fine.

My dad was right, for I stayed broke supporting that old car.
An empty wallet and no gas for me were shooting par.
Yet, every now and then I'd have some money I had saved.
I'd drive to town for apple pie, with ice cream that I craved.
My Model "A:" took me to places close and far away,
from farms around the valley to the San Francisco Bay.
We'd travel down the highway going almost forty-five.
My friends and I all singing songs, my God, were we alive.

Then, as the summer evenings turned to fall, temptation grew.
The fields had melons by the hundreds, everybody knew;
especially all the high school boys, who had a car to drive.
A little mystery with adventure keeps young boys alive.
We'd "borrow" watermelons from the farmers that we knew.
We fished and hunted year-around; yes, that's illegal, too.
Some guys would pile into a car and cruise the fields by night.
They'd find a field away from homes; where there was not a light.
Then stop for just a moment as they sneaked into the field.
With melons under both their arms; that's all that they could wield.
Back to the car in moments, they'd escape. No harm was done.
The farmers wouldn't miss the melons, and the kids had fun.

That's how the "melon season" went; most farmers didn't care.
It's something that most boys just did, with everyone aware.
But there is always one who makes "small stuff" into a war.
On "principle" he'd stand his ground; like he's superior.
Now, we all knew exactly how he felt; that egged us on.
When we wanted excitement, the decision was foregone.

We snitched from "old man Hughes", and we took melons by the ton.
He couldn't catch us; we're too young and "smart"; we had great fun.

So, on this night with two school friends, we hopped into my car.
Then drove along the road to "old man Hughes", it wasn't far.
I slowed the car. My friends jumped out. I felt a great big "thump".
I didn't want to stop. I thought I'd simply hit a bump.
I looked into my rear-view mirror; I saw what I had hit.
My friend was lying on the road; he didn't move a bit.
The "rules" were "out the window" as I quickly stopped my "A".
Ran back to see what I had done; my mind in disarray!
And as I ran up to his body lying on the ground,
I heard him breathing, and a groan; there was no other sound.

My "knobby tire print" was visible, across his chest.
He stirred, and then got to his feet, in awe, I stood, impressed!
He brushed his shirt and with my other friend, then jumped the fence.
I ran back to my "A", drove on; at first it made no sense.
And, then I realized the change I'd made early that day.
For I was always making little changes to my "A".
The "running boards" had been removed. I hadn't told a soul.
Replacing them with a "roll bar" had been my only goal.
This night, my friend stepped out; his foot went right down to the ground.
He fell under the car, and took the fall, without a sound.
My "model A" was light, so when it rolled over his chest,
it dirtied up his shirt a bit; no damage to the rest.
So, as I drove my "A" on down the road to turn around.
They stacked some melons by the fence; huge melons they had found.

110

I slowly drove back down the road; they pitched the melons in.
My "model A" sputtered and coughed; no sound from the engine.
I tried the starter; nope; I tried the crank; it wouldn't start.
The lights came on in the Hughes house; we'd soon have to depart.
And from the house we heard the shouting; front door slamming shut.
We pushed the "A" fast as we could; we almost broke a gut.
And then my friends, without a word, took off like frightened deer.
The "model A", the melons, me; the whole damned scene was queer.
I took the melons out and stacked them back along the fence.
I guess I wasn't thinking, for it didn't make much sense.
The evidence was there, my "model A" and I, alone.
Old farmer Hughes, his shotgun, and his face of "steely stone"!

I can't repeat what he said then, vernacular obscene.
The cuss words flowed incessantly, with not much in between.
He pointed that old gun at me, with threats you'd not believe.
When he got through with me; parents and friends; siblings would grieve.
I couldn't do a thing; my car won't run; my guilt is clear.
And with that gun poked in my gut, I really felt some fear.

I guess I showed enough remorse, for suddenly he quit.
I'm shaking in my boots; he's laughing like he's in a fit.
He turns and goes back to his house; I wipe my sweaty brow.
A moment, I've recovered; have to plan what I'll do now.

I look into the engine of my "A" to see what's wrong.
I smell the gas under the car; the odor is quite strong.
The line has broken from the fuel pump; all the gas is gone.
I push the "A" along the road; I've got to carry on.
It's almost morning when I get my "A" back to my house.

Embarrassed, I've been caught; I'm feeling lower than a louse.
I'm thinking I'll stay home today; not face the kids at school.
I know they'll laugh and kid me, and I'll be a perfect fool.

It doesn't take a lot of time; the valley's very small.
One neighbor calls another; then another makes a call.
And pretty soon the story's out; the whole damned valley knows.
I might as well walk naked down the street, devoid of clothes.

I pull it all together and I make my way to school.
Head hanging as I climb the stairs; I feel a perfect fool.
I find a chair, way in the back, that's on the window side,
and sit there hoping this will be a place for me to hide.
As students come into the room, some look at me with awe.
While I shrink in my chair, like I have just broken the law.

And, then the friends who left me all alone the night before,
came marching, big as life, right up the stairs and through the
door.
They're laughing, slapping backs and having one great big old
time.
I huddle down against the wall, a criminal with his crime.
My friends, with all the other students, stand around me now,
all talking of how brave I am, that what I'd done, somehow,
has set a standard for all of the students in the school,
for when to back away and when to stay and fight a rule.
The story had it that I'd stayed; I could have run away.
And facing certain danger; principles I'd not betray.
I stood my ground; argued my case; I'd won a victory.
My bravery was beyond reproach. I sat there helplessly,
as I became a hero to my other friends at school.
When all the time I'd felt that I had been a stupid fool.

The "game of whisper" as the story was told, retold some more,
Had me, small David, he Goliath, engaged in war.

I represented students, all the rules that held them back.
And, he was the "establishment"; I went on the attack.
Through me, the students won this battle, all a bit more free,
to do the things that students do, and do them happily.
A "hero" in my time, "big man" on campus, for one day!
Tomorrow? Back to normal. There is little more to say.

I kept the Model "A" till I got out of school that year.
I cherished it as an old friend, a special souvenir.
Together we had gone where other cars could never go.
And, we had shared a kind of love that most will never know.

I've owned a lot of cars as I have traveled through this life.
And, some of them were fun to own and some caused lots of strife.
But, none of them compare; there's little else that I can say.
I cherish every memory of my beat-up Model "A".

Printed in the USA
CPSIA information can be obtained
at www.ICGtesting.com
LVHW021821071223
765728LV00078B/2113

9 798887 755137